FREE RIDE
The Tax-exempt Economy

by **GILBERT M. GAUL**
and **NEILL A. BOROWSKI**
of The Philadelphia Inquirer

Andrews and McMeel
A Universal Press Syndicate Company
Kansas City

Free Ride: The Tax-exempt Economy copyright © 1993 by Gilbert M.
Gaul and Neill A. Borowski. All rights reserved. Printed in the
United States of America. No part of this book may be used or
reproduced in any manner whatsoever without written permission
except in the case of reprints in the context of reviews. For information write Andrews and McMeel, a Universal Press Syndicate
Company, 4900 Main Street, Kansas City, Missouri 64112.

Designed by Barrie Maguire

Library of Congress Cataloging-in-Publication Data

Gaul, Gilbert M.
    Free ride : the tax-exempt economy / by Gilbert M. Gaul and
Neill A. Borowski.
        p.   cm.
    Includes index.
    ISBN 0-8362-8029-6
    1. Taxation, Exemption from—United States. 2. Nonprofit
organizations—United States. I. Borowski, Neill A. II. Title.
HJ2337.U6G37   1993
336.2'06'0973—dc20   93-20930
                                                           CIP

CONTENTS

ACKNOWLEDGMENTS

Free Ride: The Tax-exempt Economy first appeared as a seven-part series in The Philadelphia Inquirer. As with many newspaper stories, it started with a deceptively simple question: What role do nonprofits play in the American economy? Before the answer to this question appeared in print, nearly two years had passed, thousands of records had been examined, more than 250 interviews had been conducted, and The Inquirer's unique commitment to exploring complicated issues had once more been affirmed.

This book would not have been possible without the support, consideration, patience, and understanding of the dedicated editors, reporters, and researchers who help to make The Inquirer a truly special place to practice journalism. They are too numerous to recount here. But rest assured their contributions do not go unnoticed. Their skill, courage, and fighting spirit resonate throughout a business that rapidly is being reduced to marketing and focus groups.

Our heartfelt thanks go out to Inquirer Editor Maxwell E.P. King, who, in the best tradition of newspaper editors, understood the importance of this subject and gave us the time and resources to report it. Max's enthusiasm for this project made our lives far easier.

The stamp of our editor, Lois Wark, appears throughout this book. Lois is a skillful editor, conscience, and friend. Her tireless work habits and unflinching commitment to this project carried us all through the long and difficult editing process. This is Lois's book as much as it is ours.

Our thanks also to our photographer, Mike Mally; copy editor Cindy Henry; graphic artist Charles Chamberlin; layout editor Bob Filarsky; our ever resourceful research librarian, Teresa Banik; research assistant Bing Mark; computer guru Al Hasbrouck; and Executive Editor Jim Naughton, whose insights aided us down the final stretch.

Special thanks to *The Inquirer*'s Business Editor, Jan Schaffer. Jan had to fare without two members of her modest staff throughout this project—no small accomplishment. Her support was unwavering.

It must also be noted that, while we were researching this project, our colleagues were working harder than ever to pick up the slack. Thank you.

A work of this length and complexity inevitably absorbs its authors. Vacations, weekends, and dinners are lost. Even when at home, one's mind is often working ahead. All of this takes a toll on spouses, children, and friends. Ours were no exceptions. Our wives, Cathryn Gaul and Charmaine Borowski, are the real heroes; without their love and support, this book would not have been possible.

Gilbert M. Gaul
Neill A. Borowski

CHAPTER 1

The profitable world of nonprofits

The National Football League, that bastion of free enterprise and million-dollar quarterbacks, doesn't look like a nonprofit organization. Then again, it doesn't act like one, either. The NFL spends less than 1 percent of its $35 million budget on charitable activities, pays its commissioner $1.5 million a year, and spends another $1.5 million to lease seven floors of a Park Avenue office tower.

Or take the Motion Picture Academy of Arts and Sciences, which spent $6 million to put on the dazzling Oscars show. You thought nonprofit organizations had to be charities, run by meagerly paid managers and volunteers?

Not anymore. Thanks to the remarkable largess of Washington lawmakers, an ever expanding definition of charity, and a near-total collapse of government supervision, America's nonprofit economy has become a huge, virtually unregulated industry.

Within it, almost anything and anybody qualifies for tax-exempt status: Auto racing promoters. Collection agencies. Country clubs. Criminals. A half-billion-dollar defense research corporation. Investment houses. Mail-order colleges. A polo museum. Retail stores. Professional surfers. An association of Druids. Foreign real estate investors. Space explorers. Even a chili appreciation society.

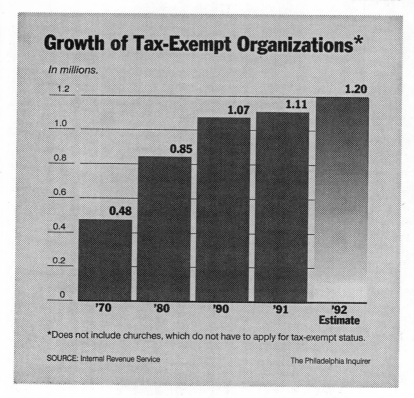

Growth of Tax-Exempt Organizations*

In millions.

1.2

1.20

1.11

1.07

1.0

0.85

0.8

0.6

0.48

0.4

0.2

0

'70   '80   '90   '91   '92
Estimate

*Does not include churches, which do not have to apply for tax-exempt status.

SOURCE: Internal Revenue Service   The Philadelphia Inquirer

Each year since the start of the 1980s, an average of twenty-nine thousand new groups have been declared nonprofit and gone off the tax rolls. Today, an estimated 1.2 million organizations are exempt from taxes—not counting churches, which don't even have to apply.

Think of it as Congress's contribution to charity. And you make up for the taxes they don't pay.

A major but little-noticed change has taken place in the American economy in the last twenty years: the dramatic growth of nonprofit businesses. These businesses had an estimated $500 billion in revenues in 1990—nearly six times the income of farms, five times that of utilities, and twice as much as the construction industry. They represented roughly 6 percent of the nation's total economic output and employed about seven million people.

Since 1970, this tax-exempt sector has grown four times as

fast as the rest of the economy. In Philadelphia, for example, nonprofits account for one of every six jobs among private employers. From the University of Pennsylvania, with 1991 revenues of $1.3 billion, to the Sonny Hill community basketball league, with revenues of $279,000, nonprofits affect the lives of Philadelphians in untold ways. Nonprofit hospitals, universities, museums, and churches own large parcels of real estate, on which they pay no property or income taxes. Even the most dramatic building on the Philadelphia skyline, One Liberty Place, was built with financing help from a nonprofit pension fund.

Nationally, nonprofits control property, cash, and investments worth more than $850 billion—and that is a conservative estimate. Because neither churches nor smaller nonprofit groups have to report income or assets, the true figure probably exceeds $1 trillion. Government economists acknowledge that they don't track the tax-free economy or its impact.

To put $850 billion in perspective: If the holdings of nonprofit groups and foundations were liquidated tomorrow, there would be enough to write a $3,401 check for each man, woman, and child in America. Or enough to pay off last year's federal deficit and have more than $500 billion left over.

These exemptions are costing more than $36.5 billion a year in lost tax revenue—at a time when President Clinton is asking Americans to shoulder an increasing tax burden. That is the equivalent of the income taxes paid by the twenty-five million taxpayers whose income is between $12,000 and $25,000.

At the local level, the exclusion of billions of dollars worth of property from the tax rolls of cash-starved school districts and municipalities is increasing budget woes and straining social services.

The transformation of this nonprofit economy has happened largely without notice, forethought, or national debate about the consequences and public policy implications for the country.

Nonprofit groups do a lot of good in a lot of areas for a lot of people. That's why they were granted exemption from taxation. But as Congress has become more and more generous with the nonprofit designation, and as the Internal Revenue Service has become swamped, abuses have grown.

An eighteen-month study by The Philadelphia Inquirer, which included examination of tax returns of six thousand exempt organizations, found that:

▪ Many nonprofits operate just like for-profit businesses. They make huge profits, pay handsome salaries, build office towers, invest billions of dollars in stocks and bonds, employ lobbyists, and use political action committees to influence legislation. And increasingly they compete with taxpaying businesses.

▪ Executives at some large nonprofit businesses make more than $1 million a year. Of twenty-five thousand salaries of executives of big nonprofit organizations that were examined, nearly half were at least $100,000 a year. The top compensation in 1991 was NFL commissioner Paul Tagliabue, who was paid $1,511,731 in salary and benefits. Many also received such perks as free housing, maid service, luxury cars and chauffeurs, and no-interest loans.

▪ Nonprofit hospitals, which originally were exempted from taxes because of their charity care, now devote an average of 6 percent of expenditures to caring for the poor. Meanwhile, more than $1 billion in hospital profits have been shifted to commercial spinoffs—hotels, restaurants, health spas, laundries, marinas, parking garages.

▪ Private, nonprofit colleges and universities have more than doubled their tuition in the last decade, even though their income from investments was doubling and tripling in the 1980s. Some schools—including MIT, Cal Tech, and Penn State's main campus—now spend more on research than on teaching; these schools collect millions of dollars for work done under contract to commercial companies. This income is shielded from taxes, and the companies get a tax write-off.

▪ Private foundations have become great warehouses of untaxed wealth. Most foundations give away only the minimum required by law, 5 percent of their assets each year, while earning much more on investments. With $163 billion in assets, they are operated like private banks, with elite, self-perpetuating boards of directors. Where they invest their money and how they vote their stock give these boards great economic power.

▪ A multibillion-dollar pool of cheap money, available through low-interest loans to tax-exempt organizations and subsidized by taxpayers, has financed a massive expansion of hospitals and universities. Some have overbuilt: On any given night, one-third of the hospital beds in America are empty. In Pennsylvania, more than one hundred government authorities issue low-interest tax-exempt bonds, with few questions about whether the projects are needed.

■ Dozens of directors and executives of nonprofit institutions own or are officers of outside companies that do business with the nonprofits they run. The services they provide range from legal and financial advice to selling the nonprofit food or other goods. The IRS requires disclosure of such relationships but only minimal details about finances.

■ The Internal Revenue Service, which is charged with policing nonprofits, is so understaffed—and the number of exempt organizations so large—that it would take seventy-nine years to audit them all at the present rate. Most applications for nonprofit status are rubber-stamped by IRS; even convicted felons have been approved.

"Until I looked, I thought being declared a nonprofit was pretty hard. Then I found something like 95 or 99 percent who apply get approved. It's like getting your driver's license," said Ted Chapler, executive director of the Iowa Finance Authority, which arranges tax-exempt financing for nonprofit organizations.

Don't be misled by the word "nonprofit." It does not mean these groups cannot earn a profit on their services. They make plenty of profit—although they don't call it that.

Under the federal tax code, nonprofit businesses may accumulate net income, so long as they don't distribute it as dividends or stock. Where does the money go then? In many cases, to expand their empires. That means to build new buildings, expand services, acquire competitors, increase executive salaries, and hire high-priced consultants, among other things.

"I call it the culture of the nonprofit," said Princeton University economist Uwe Reinhart. "You can't keep the money for yourself, right, so you do the next best thing. You put up another building or give yourself a raise. As a nonprofit, who's going to question this?"

As they've expanded, many large nonprofit organizations have moved beyond their core mission into commercial businesses that have little, if anything, to do with their exempt purpose.

Under the tax code, nonprofits are allowed to operate commercial subsidiaries—so long as they pay taxes on that income, and so long as those activities don't overshadow their exempt mission.

Cost of Tax Breaks for Nonprofits
(billions of dollars)

$36.5 billion a year . . . .

Deductions for charitable donations	**$18.0**
Nonprofit hospitals	
• Federal income tax	**$4.5**
• State and local taxes	**$3.5**
Colleges and Universities	**$4.0**
Foundations	**$4.0**
Tax-exempt bonds	**$2.0**
Postage discount	**$0.5**

Total does not include: Local property taxes, state or city sales taxes, taxes waived for churches and religious groups

Layers of Tax Breaks
Tax-exempt groups benefit in many ways

Philadelphia • Property tax • Business tax • Sales tax

Pennsylvania • Income tax • Sales tax • Insurance premium tax

United States • Income tax • Capital gains tax • Postage discount

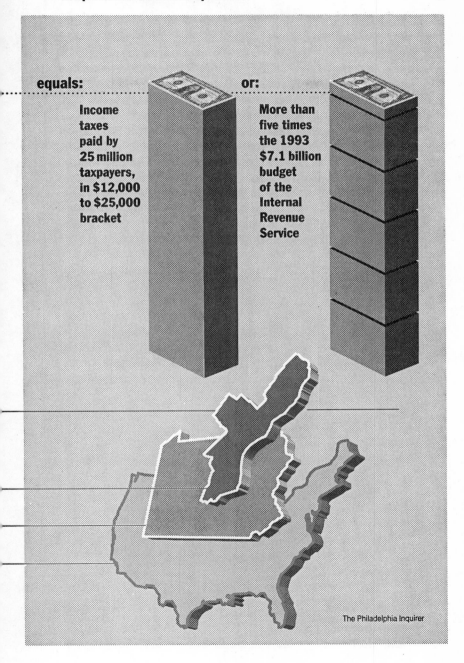

equals:

Income
taxes
paid by
25 million
taxpayers,
in $12,000
to $25,000
bracket

or:

More than
five times
the 1993
$7.1 billion
budget
of the
Internal
Revenue
Service

The Philadelphia Inquirer

"The idea that tax-exempt organizations always wear white hats in the community, going around doing things that benefit everyone and helping the poor . . . as opposed to that other part of society that gropes for money all day long, is not something that is rooted in fact," Marcus S. Owens, director of the IRS's Exempt Organizations Technical Division, told nonprofit officials in a candid 1991 speech.

Originally, tax exemption was granted to groups that relieved the government of having to provide a service—schools, hospitals, social service agencies, and the like. The law limited tax-exempt status to charitable institutions. which received their funds mostly from private donors.

There are still many small nonprofits staffed by volunteers and low-paid workers that provide needed services to their communities. But over the years, three basic changes have occurred with large nonprofits. Instead of depending on charitable contributions, many tax-exempt businesses began charging fees for services. And the fees kept rising. Also, federal programs—Medicaid, Medicare, Social Security disability—began paying for many of the services once provided by charities. And Congress, responding to special interests, expanded its definition of nonprofit to include many new categories, such as fraternal groups, trade associations, mutual life insurance companies, health insurance firms, labor unions, retirement funds, cemeteries, and credit unions.

Today, there are 25 categories of nonprofits—including the one that covers the NFL.

Congress rewrote the tax laws in 1966 to declare the professional football league a not-for-profit enterprise, inserting the NFL in the same section of the tax code that exempts boards of trade and local chambers of commerce from federal taxes. The exemption covers only the league organization, not the teams and players within it.

Nor is the NFL the only professional sports organization to benefit. The National Hockey League, Professional Bowling Association, Professional Golf Association, U.S. Tennis Association and the players' associations of football and major league baseball are among the many tax-exempt sports groups.

Then there's the National Museum of Polo & Hall of Fame. Its exempt purpose "relates to the operation of the Polo Museum and Hall of Fame at the Kentucky Horse Park in Lexington, Ky." Among its major 1990 expenses: tent rental, catering, and dinner at the Club Collette in Palm Beach, Florida.

I n January 1993, officials at Memorial Sloan-Kettering Cancer Center in New York mailed a plea for funds for cancer research. "Right now, cancer research is being threatened by cutbacks in federal funding of research. This could seriously hinder our efforts to find more effective treatments and cures," said a "Special Note" to would-be contributors.

The note did not say that Sloan-Kettering is one of the wealthiest hospitals in the nation, with more than $500 million in cash and investments. Or that the renowned cancer facility had more than $250 million in reserves available for any purpose, including research. Or that the center is the sole beneficiary of a $92 million trust fund, which underwrites research at an affiliated laboratory. Sloan-Kettering is a prime example of how wealthy some nonprofits have become, while continuing to solicit contributions.

"Our reserves are substantial," Mortimer H. Chute, Jr., Sloan-Kettering's $195,000-a-year vice-president for development, acknowledged in an interview. But, he said, "we want to do more things. We need private philanthropy to greatly expand our research efforts."

Chute said that Sloan-Kettering's federal research funding had not "kept pace with inflation, with the Consumer Price Index." He did not have specifics, and officials did not respond to requests for that information.

In 1990, Sloan-Kettering spent $8.1 million on fund-raising and received contributions and pledges totaling $59.3 million, according to its IRS tax filing. It made $27 million in profit, which nonprofits call a surplus. That was down from $54 million a year earlier. This is big business, by anybody's definition.

For most companies, earning ten cents in profit on every dollar in revenue would be considered a very good year. Many large nonprofits make that much and more.

In 1991, the University of Pennsylvania made eleven cents in profit for each dollar it took in—$153 million profit on revenues of $1.3 billion. A year before, it made thirteen cents on the dollar. During most of the 1980s, Penn enjoyed double-digit profit margins.

Princeton University has done even better. In 1990, it made

Who's a nonprofit? Here are a few examples

	National Hockey League	MITRE Corp.	National Rifle Association
LOCATION:	Montreal	Bedford, Mass.	Washington
PURPOSE:	Runs professional hockey league	Engineering services for government	Lobbies, publishes magazines, supports gun owners
REVENUES:	$12 million in 1990	$572 million in 1991	$86 million in 1990
PROFIT:	$0	$8 million	$399,200
ASSETS:	$0	$103 million	$11 million
PRESIDENT:	John A. Ziegler, paid $500,000; received $300,000 no-interest loan to buy a house	Barry M. Horowitz, paid $267,168	Joe Foss, not paid
OF NOTE:	Listed European scouting ($165,418) and Hockey Hall of Fame ($255,000) as expenses	Helped to develop AWACS and other defense industry surveillance systems	Owned $89 million in investments, has Political Action Committee

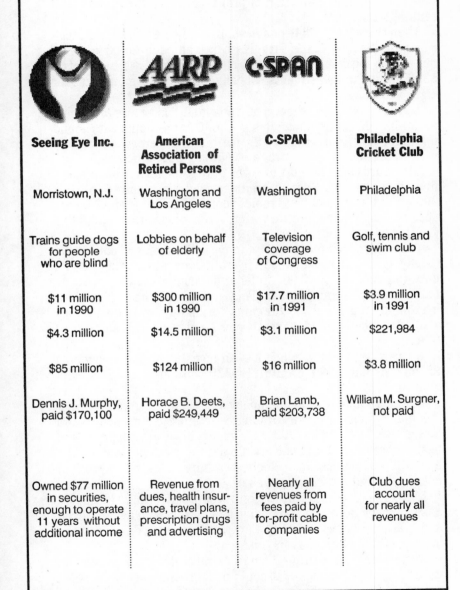

Seeing Eye Inc.	American Association of Retired Persons	C-SPAN	Philadelphia Cricket Club
Morristown, N.J.	Washington and Los Angeles	Washington	Philadelphia
Trains guide dogs for people who are blind	Lobbies on behalf of elderly	Television coverage of Congress	Golf, tennis and swim club
$11 million in 1990	$300 million in 1990	$17.7 million in 1991	$3.9 million in 1991
$4.3 million	$14.5 million	$3.1 million	$221,984
$85 million	$124 million	$16 million	$3.8 million
Dennis J. Murphy, paid $170,100	Horace B. Deets, paid $249,449	Brian Lamb, paid $203,738	William M. Surgner, not paid
Owned $77 million in securities, enough to operate 11 years without additional income	Revenue from dues, health insurance, travel plans, prescription drugs and advertising	Nearly all revenues from fees paid by for-profit cable companies	Club dues account for nearly all revenues

thirty-two cents profit on every dollar of revenue—$197 million on revenues of about $613 million. Only one public company, Newmont Mining, had a higher profit margin in the *Fortune* 500 rankings that year.

Then there's the Bible business. In 1991, the nonprofit American Bible Society made fifty-five cents on each dollar of revenue—$52 million on revenues of $95 million. The Society's $350 million in investments was enough to run the business for eight years.

As these examples show, many nonprofit businesses are highly profitable. A computer analysis of 630 large nonprofits found that they had an average profit margin of 9 percent in 1990— more than double the average of *Fortune* 500 companies.

All figures are based on Form 990 returns the businesses filed with the IRS. Exempt organizations are required to file a 990, even if they had no taxable income. The filing requirement does not apply to nonprofits with revenue of less than $25,000 a year, or to churches.

These big profit margins are, in part, the result of not having to pay taxes. If these were for-profit companies, they would have to pay up to $340,000 in federal income taxes for every $1 million in operating income. They also would be subject to a maximum 28 percent capital gains tax on any investments they sold. And they would have to pay local property, sales, and other taxes.

Harvard University, which has an investment portfolio worth $5 billion, had 1990 profits of $230 million—a 17.5 percent margin.

Not every nonprofit made money. Mt. Sinai Hospital in Philadelphia, a division of the Graduate Health System, recorded a loss of $16.8 million in 1990. As a group, however, hospitals and health-care organizations were among the most profitable. The Mayo Clinic Foundation in Rochester, Minnesota, had a profit of nearly $90 million on revenues of $642 million.

Mayo's 14 percent profit margin would have ranked it ahead of such pharmaceutical companies as Johnson & Johnson, Pfizer, and Warner Lambert. And the drug industry is considered the most profitable business in America.

Mayo was so wealthy, it ended 1991 with $979 million in unrestricted funds, money it could use for whatever it chose. It operated eleven taxable subsidiaries, including an airport management company, and had twenty-eight companies in all. Mayo owned buildings, property, and equipment valued at $773 million, including spinoff clinics in Jacksonville, Florida, and Scottsdale, Arizona.

Another charity that fared well was Father Flanagan's Boys Home, better known as Boys Town, near Omaha, Nebraska. In fiscal 1989, it had a profit of $29 million on income of $93 million—a 31 percent margin. That would have dwarfed margins of IBM, General Motors, Reebok, or Time-Warner.

Boys Town, popularized in a 1938 film featuring Spencer Tracy and Mickey Rooney, owned stocks, bonds, property, and Treasury bills worth nearly $423 million. It had four outside advisers to manage its investment portfolio.

In 1990, Boys Town officials set up a separate tax-exempt foundation, Father Flanagan's Foundation Fund, and transferred $371 million in investment holdings. Since then, the value of the foundation's holdings has increased to $478 million.

Boys Town's treasurer, Jim Schmidt, said the goal was to build up the foundation's endowment and use a portion of the interest income to help support Boys Town's expanding services to troubled children.

During the Civil Rights era, the struggling Southern Poverty Law Center in Montgomery, Alabama, battled poll taxes, racism, and the Ku Klux Klan. Today, it, too, is building up cash reserves. Thanks to an aggressive fund-raising campaign, the law center made forty-five cents in profit on each dollar in revenue it took in during 1990—$4.5 million on $10 million in revenue. The year before it made fifty-nine cents on the dollar.

These days, the center spends more on education than on lawsuits. "When we started out in the '60s, we were the only ones down here in the South taking on these issues," said executive director Morris Dees. "Nowadays, it's no longer hard for other lawyers to take these cases. . . . It's a natural outgrowth, moving from the courtroom to the classroom."

The center's investment holdings were $44 million as of July 1992. "Our goal is to build toward a time where we won't be dependent on direct mail appeals, a time we will be totally self-sufficient," Dees said. "We believe $100 million in endowment will be enough."

The Pennsylvania Horticultural Society is also building its bank account. Thanks to its generous donors and the $1 million profit it usually makes sponsoring the Philadelphia Flower Show, the nonprofit group's investment holdings grew from $4.5 million in 1989 to $6.1 million in 1992.

In March 1993, a blizzard forced the flower show to close early the final weekend, cutting profits by half—or $510,000. The society put out a call for donations.

"As you can well imagine, the losses caused by the blizzard are devastating," a fund-raising letter said. Tax-exempt donations would "be used to cover the costs of providing uninterrupted PHS programs," such as the Philadelphia Green neighborhood gardens, the letter said.

The Horticultural Society could have gone into its $6.1 million reserves to make up the shortfall.

"We look at that not as a reserve but as an endowment which this year and future years is going to provide income. So if you dip into that, then you lose income in the future," said society president Jane G. Pepper.

Congress has not placed limits on the profits that tax-exempt groups may make. Nor has it addressed whether there should be limits on their investment portfolios. Absent such rules, all the IRS can do is try to "track where the money is going," IRS's Owens said.

The impact of this expanding tax-exempt industry is being felt throughout America.

In such Pennsylvania counties as Beaver, Montour, Lehigh, Lawrence, and Lycoming, the largest employer isn't a private company, it's a nonprofit hospital.

In cities like Philadelphia, nonprofits dominate the job market. In 1992, eight of the ten biggest employers in Philadelphia County paid no property or income taxes. They were either government agencies or nonprofit organizations, like the University of Pennsylvania, Temple University, and Thomas Jefferson University. The only taxpaying companies among the ten biggest employers were Bell of Pennsylvania and Philadelphia National Bank.

In the Philadelphia, South Jersey, and Delaware region last year, nonprofits brought in revenues exceeding $18 billion. That $18 billion—virtually all of it untaxed—was more than the

Top 10 Employers in Philadelphia

8 out of 10 pay no property taxes

RANK	EMPLOYER	EMPLOYMENT
1	**U.S. Government**	52,940
2	**City of Philadelphia**	30,926
3	**Philadelphia School District**	30,532
4	**University of Pennsylvania**	16,645
5	**Temple University**	9,902
6	**Thomas Jefferson University**	8,807
7	**SEPTA (transit agency)**	7,061
8	Bell of Pennsylvania	6,555
9	**Hahnemann University**	5,065
10	Philadelphia National Bank	4,970

Boldface denotes institutions that do not pay taxes

SOURCE: Pa. Department of Labor and Industry   The Philadelphia Inquirer

state budget for New Jersey. It was more than the combined revenues of Campbell Soup, Scott Paper, and Philadelphia Electric Company.

In Pennsylvania alone, twenty thousand charitable groups in 1991 took in $33 billion—up from $20 billion in 1985. That six-year growth rate of 65 percent was more than double the rate of inflation. And that was just charities; the figure doesn't include an estimated sixty thousand other tax-exempt groups.

In Cambria County, seven of the ten biggest employers in 1990 were government agencies or nonprofit groups. Bethlehem Steel ranked as the number one employer, but the company is preparing to shut down its Bar, Rod and Wire Division in Johnstown.

If that happens, the area's most important source of jobs would be three nonprofit hospitals.

Many nonprofits defend their tax-exempt privilege by citing their economic contributions to their communities.
In January 1992, the University of Pennsylvania released a university-financed study reporting that Penn "contributes at least $2.5 billion to the state's economy—including $1 billion to household earnings—and supports more than 40,000 jobs in the state."

The Delaware Valley Hospital Council hired the Pennsylvania Economy League to measure the economic impact of its member hospitals. "Our hospitals employ more than 72,000 people. Salaries and wages alone add about $2 billion annually to the economy and about $60 million to the city [Philadelphia] in wage tax," President Jeff Flood said in 1991.

Such economic power is important. But it has nothing to do with why hospitals, universities, or other nonprofits were exempted from taxes. Those reasons have to do with their charitable and social missions, not the jobs they create.

Otherwise, department stores and pizza parlors would be tax-exempt, too.

In some tax-strapped communities, nonprofits' growing wealth and economic power are now drawing attention to their privileges. In 1989, officials in Pittsburgh and surrounding Allegheny County, Pennsylvania, began threatening to tax nonprofit organizations. Since then, some hospitals, a blood bank, and a YMCA have agreed to make annual payments in lieu of taxes.

In Philadelphia, the Board of Revision of Taxes recently rejected applications for tax exemptions on new property owned by the nonprofit American Red Cross's Penn-Jersey Regional Blood Services and the National Board of Medical Examiners, saying these groups did not serve a charitable purpose. The mayor's office is studying whether to seek payments in lieu of taxes from hospitals, universities, and other nonprofits.

In financially strapped Johnstown, Pennsylvania, Mayor Herb Pfuhl in 1992 called publicly on Conemaugh Valley Memorial Hospital to pay its share of taxes. Hospital officials responded with an offer to provide some health services free and to donate police and fire gear. Pfuhl rejected the offer, saying, "It will not relieve the burden of the average taxpayer."

In Langhorne Borough, Bucks County, a Philadelphia suburb, officials amended the township's zoning ordinance in 1991 to limit "property devoted to tax-exempt or nontaxable uses" to 25 percent of the borough's total acreage. A borough attorney said the ordinance was designed to prevent any further erosion of the tax base.

In 1991, officials in Wayne County, Pennsylvania, voted to put back on the property tax rolls more than one thousand acres owned by three New York-based summer camps. Their reasoning: Because the camps charged fees, they weren't charities. Attorneys for the camps appealed to the county court, then to Commonwealth Court—and lost at both levels.

In 1988, Erie County, Pennsylvania, officials revoked the tax-exempt status of the 536-bed Hamot Medical Center, one of the area's largest employers. The county said that after a 1981 corporate reorganization, Hamot had shifted $25 million in hospital profits to a holding company and subsidiaries involved in real estate development and other commercial ventures, including a marina on Lake Erie.

Hamot officials filed suit, and a trial was held in Erie County's Court of Common Pleas. In May 1990, Judge George Levin ruled that the Hamot executives had "lost their identity" as hospital officials, "and their dominant purpose was no longer the promotion of health, but to fund HHSI [Hamot's parent organization] and its various subsidiaries."

Levin upheld the county's decision to tax Hamot and its affiliates. The hospital appealed to Commonwealth Court and lost there, too. In June 1992, Hamot's board of directors announced that it would cease operations of many of the subsidiaries and again focus on health care.

"We have an obligation to the patients and the more than 2,500 people who work at Hamot to carry out our mission in a way that responds to community expectations for nonprofits," Hamot chairman Bruce Raimy said.

In July 1992, state senator Michael E. Bortner of York introduced a bill allowing Pennsylvania cities to levy service charges on some tax-exempt properties. The measure was designed to help cities in which there are large numbers of nonprofit organizations.

"This has eroded the tax base and forced home owners and small businesses to carry the total burden of supporting municipal government services," Bortner said in introducing the bill.

"Taxes are the lifeblood of government and no taxpayer should be permitted to escape the payment of his just share," Judge Levin wrote in his Hamot opinion.

Yet an examination by *The Philadelphia Inquirer* of the way the federal government awards tax-exempt status shows it amounts to little more than a rubber stamp. The Exempt Organizations Technical Division of the IRS receives thousands of applications each year for exemption.

At a June 1988 hearing of the House Committee on Small Business, a Treasury Department official was asked about the ever-expanding categories of nonprofits. "It would seem almost irreversible," Assistant Treasury Secretary Adelbert L. Spitzer replied. "There are currently twenty-five categories of exempt organizations. It presents problems."

"Is it possible that we should be looking at the basic definition of . . . what should be tax-exempt? And try to really minimize the number of categories, tighten up the definition?" Representative James R. Olin of Virginia inquired.

"We think the subject is certainly worth exploring and is a review we have recommended Congress undertake," Spitzer responded.

But Congress didn't follow through. It has not examined the basic issue of who qualifies for tax-exempt status since 1969.

Meanwhile, the IRS moves the applications through. In 1990, the most recent year for which figures were available, the IRS rejected 656, while approving 38,649. Applicants had a one-in-sixty chance of *not* being approved. In 1980, the rejection rate was one-in-twenty-seven applicants.

The application asks a series of questions, such as the names and addresses of the organization's incorporators and what charitable activities they intend to conduct. So long as the applicants fill in reasonable answers and pay a $375 filing fee, there is little chance of being rejected.

"We accept as truthful the statements the applicants make on the application," said the IRS's Owens.

There have been any number of abuses. Take the case of Edwin E. Whitis II, a forty-three-year-old Texan with a history of legal troubles. In 1988, the Austin IRS office approved an application submitted by Whitis; his wife, Deanna; and a Rev. Harvey Couts seeking tax exemption to operate a national charity for abused and battered children.

Rev. Couts, it turned out, did not exist. When federal officials went looking for him, the only person they could find by that name had been dead for five years.

On the December 31, 1987, application, the Whitises said they planned to raise money through television ads, direct-mail appeals, and by operating bingo games and holding car washes and other neighborhood drives. The money would assist abused children at their ranch and "build a 500-bed medical facility for the seriously injured child."

Based on his past, Ed Whitis seemed like an unusual choice to operate a charity for children. Police and court records in Texas show that Whitis had been arrested on eight occasions between 1970 and 1977 on charges ranging from forgery and stealing credit cards to possession of heroin. He had received probation on the heroin charge and later served two years in federal prison on a conviction in a check-writing scheme involving stolen mail. In the early 1980s, Whitis served a second prison term on separate charges of theft and forgery.

About the time his application for America's Battered Children was being reviewed by the IRS in 1988, Whitis was involved in a scam that bilked investors out of $3.2 million, according to federal court records. Whitis pleaded guilty following a 1988 fraud indictment that said he and three others took millions of dollars in "advance fees" from borrowers without arranging any loans. He was sentenced to five and a half years in federal prison.

How could someone like Whitis slip by the IRS to earn tax-payer-subsidized charity status? "Nobody ever asked me about my past," Whitis said by phone from prison in Oakdale, Louisiana. "You don't have to submit a resume or anything, and the application doesn't take that into account. They don't even ask if you have a criminal past. If they had, I would have told them. I wouldn't have tried to hide it."

Indeed, the IRS application for tax exemption, known as Form 1023, does not ask whether the applicant has been convicted of a crime. Owens said such a question wasn't needed, because not many criminals apply.

Whitis insisted that America's Battered Children was not a scam. "I don't want anyone to think we had the wrong intentions because of my past misdeeds."

Only after Whitis's indictment became public did IRS audit the books of America's Battered Children. The agent discovered a number of unusual things. The charity's assets consisted of $433,282 in cash and 375 gold bars, valued at $175,000. One of its major transactions involved the purchase, for $223,541, of a ranch the Whitises had bought for $174,500 about eighteen months earlier.

As directors of America's Battered Children, the Whitises authorized $75,292 in improvements to the ranch. These included $6,043 for draperies, $11,374 on an atrium, $3,395 on landscaping, $6,866 on carpeting, and nearly $33,000 on carpentry.

On March 7, 1991, the IRS revoked the nonprofit status of America's Battered Children, retroactive to December 31, 1987. From prison, Whitis is appealing.

Once an organization is declared tax-exempt by the IRS, it usually can piggyback other tax exemptions onto the federal one. It can seek exemption from local property taxes, state corporate income taxes, and sales taxes and can borrow money from hundreds of quasi-public authorities that issue tax-exempt bonds. The bonds carry lower interest rates than conventional loans, and the buyers are exempted from taxes on interest they earn.

Nonprofits also can apply for reduced postal rates. In 1992, nonprofit groups saved an estimated $500 million using discounted mail.

No one has the foggiest idea what all these local, state, and federal exemptions cost taxpayers. "Historically, an estimate of the impact has never been done. It goes back to when the federal income tax was first enacted in 1913; no one thought to include such an estimate," an economist at the United States Treasury said.

The Inquirer's calculations—based on budget estimates, congressional hearing records, and interviews with economists—suggest the cost is more than $36 billion a year.

And that's conservative.

Start with the subsidy for the nation's thirty-two hundred nonprofit hospitals. The General Accounting Office, Congress's financial watchdog, estimates that the Treasury loses at least $4.5 billion in income taxes on these hospitals. State and local governments lose an additional $3.5 billion.

Nonprofit colleges and universities avoid an estimated $4 billion in taxes.

Foundations have investment income on which they avoid payment of about $4 billion in federal income taxes. Add the taxes lost by exempting the interest income earned by those who buy tax-exempt bonds. The Treasury estimates that figure is more than $2 billion a year.

Now add federal income deductions taken by people who donate to universities, United Way, and other charities. Federal budget estimates put that figure at $18 billion this year. Include the federal subsidy on mailings: about $500 million a year.

That comes to $36.5 billion a year.

The actual value of the tax exemptions is much higher. There is no way to estimate the national totals for such things as property taxes or state and local sales taxes that most nonprofits avoid paying. Nor does the $36.5 billion include taxes waived for churches and religious groups, on which there are no reliable data.

Property tax records in Philadelphia show that the Archdiocese of Philadelphia, the largest religious property owner, holds at least $225 million in tax-exempt land and buildings, based on estimated market value. That does not include many parochial schools and colleges.

The value of the holdings of other religious denominations is harder to determine because no central organization owns them. But, based on the best information available, it is estimated at more than $400 million.

The largest nonprofit property owner in the city is the University of Pennsylvania, which owns land and buildings with an estimated market value of about $300 million. Temple University has about $275 million worth.

In all, at least $3.6 billion worth of property is owned by nonprofit groups in Philadelphia. If property taxes were paid on it, Philadelphia would receive about $95 million a year. And that is just one city.

States are under no obligation to grant tax exemptions just because the federal government has. But most states and local governments do.

Once in place, federal exemptions are rarely revoked—so rarely that government regulators don't keep track. At a congressional hearing on hospitals in 1991, Treasury and IRS officials were asked how many of the thirty-two hundred nonprofit hospitals nationwide had lost their tax-exempt standing in the last twenty years or so. Michael J. Graetz, deputy assistant secretary of the Treasury, replied: "It's a handful of revocations, as I understand it. I think it's more than one, but certainly less than a dozen."

A minute or two later, Graetz updated his estimate. "I think the answer . . . is five, but I was not certain of it," he said.

Still later in the hearing, assistant IRS commissioner John E. Burke offered a lower estimate: One.

Today, nonprofit organizations can be found running vacation travel tours, selling medical equipment, publishing magazines, hawking artwork or T-shirts or jewelry, developing retirement villages, selling life and health insurance, sponsoring business seminars, marketing videos, operating pharmacies, running testing services, and managing investment firms.

The IRS relies on them to report and pay taxes on any income and profits earned on businesses that are unrelated to their core charitable mission. The IRS calls this Unrelated Business Income (UBI).

In 1987, the most recent year for which IRS had detailed data, tax-exempt organizations reported $2.5 billion in gross income from unrelated business. About 60 percent of the groups said they had lost money on their business operations. The remainder reported $283 million in taxable profits, on which they paid income tax of $83 million.

The growing commercialism of nonprofits can be tracked in IRS data: Total taxes paid on their commercial business increased 379 percent—from $38 million to $182 million—between 1984 and 1992. Based on their audits, IRS officials say this kind of income is often underreported. "I don't think there's any question many tax-exempt organizations have become extraordinarily businesslike, doing things akin to the commercial sector," Owens said.

As executives of nonprofits see it, they've been forced to start for-profit businesses to provide revenue to run their exempt operations.

Their taxpaying competitors, though, say nonprofits are not merely protecting existing operations but expanding into new

Types of Tax-exempt Groups

Figures refer to sections of the U.S. Tax Code.

501 (c) (1) Corporations organized under an act of Congress.

501 (c) (2) Title-holding companies.

501 (c) (3) Charitable, educational, literary, religious, scientific organizations; organizations to prevent cruelty to animals, to prevent cruelty to children, for public safety testing.

501 (c) (4) Social welfare; civic leagues; associations of employees.

501 (c) (5) Labor, agricultural, horticultural organizations.

501 (c) (6) Business leagues; boards of trade; chambers of commerce; real estate boards.

501 (c) (7) Social and recreational clubs.

501 (c) (8) Fraternal beneficiary societies.

501 (c) (9) Voluntary employees' beneficiary societies.

501 (c) (10) Fraternal beneficiary societies.

501 (c) (11) Teachers' retirement fund.

501 (c) (12) Benevolent life insurance associations; Mutual Ditch or Irrigation Co.; Mutual Cooperative Telephone Co.

501 (c) (13) Cemetery companies, burial associations.

501 (c) (14) Credit unions.

501 (c) (15) Mutual insurance companies.

501 (c) (16) Corporations to finance crop operations.

501 (c) (17) Supplemental unemployment benefit trusts.

501 (c) (18) Employee-funded pension trust.

501 (c) (19) War veterans' organizations.

501 (c) (20) Legal services organizations.

501 (c) (21) Black lung trusts.

501 (c) (23) Veterans association (formed before 1880).

501 (c) (25) Title-holding company for pensions.

501 (d) Religious and apostolic organizations.

501 (e) Cooperative hospital service organizations.

501 (f) Cooperative service organizations of operating educational organizations.

501 (k) Child-care organization.

521 Farmers' cooperatives.

4947 (a) (2) Nonexempt charitable trust.

SOURCE: Internal Revenue Service

businesses. Moreover, taxpaying competitors complain, nonprofit businesses have unfair advantages. If a for-profit company in New Jersey spends $500,000 on new equipment or furnishings, it pays a 6 percent sales tax, or $30,000. A nonprofit buying the same equipment pays no tax.

Such advantages have helped nonprofits gain a foothold in some businesses that have been dominated by private taxpaying firms—fitness centers, for instance.

For years, fitness centers and spas were the domain of private companies. But in the 1980s, nonprofit hospitals invested more than $500 million in such centers as they sought to develop new revenue sources.

"Every time a center like this opens, it takes away potential members from for-profit facilities like my own," said Frank J. Napolitano, Jr. "We can't possibly compete fairly because they don't pay taxes and aren't regulated the same way we are. It's an enormous advantage." Napolitano is the president of Sports Club Management, a company in East Stroudsburg, Pennsylvania, that operates health clubs in Philadelphia, in Bucks County, and in five other locations.

In January 1993, Napolitano came across a newspaper advertisement for The Achievement Center, a "state-of-the-art fitness facility" near his Bucks County club. The center is affiliated with the Medical College Hospitals, a tax-exempt Philadelphia hospital group.

"I was shocked at how arrogant they were about what they were doing. Then I got angry," he said, "and I wrote them a letter asking how they justified competing with a taxpaying company. I never got a response."

The center says its programs are geared toward patients undergoing therapy. "Truth be told, we subsidize this program. We don't make money. It's part of our outreach to the community," said Meg McGoldrick, an official of Medical College Hospitals.

Commercial activities of nonprofits extend to their tax-exempt services, too. Yale economist and tax attorney Henry Hansmann, one of the nation's authorities on nonprofit organizations, has coined a term for such groups. He calls them "commercial nonprofits."

"These are nonprofits that derive substantially all of their income simply from the prices they charge for the goods and services they produce, and receive no meaningful donative support," Hansmann said at a 1987 congressional hearing.

Nonprofit Commercialism on the Rise

Taxes paid on for-profit activities.

Revenues Collected
In millions of dollars.

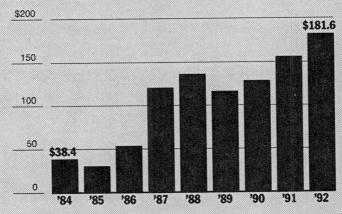

Number of Returns Filed
In thousands.

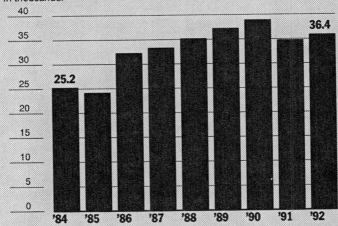

SOURCE: Internal Revenue Service, Unrelated Business Income Tax   The Philadelphia Inquirer

Hansmann has recommended that Congress consider revoking the exemptions of these fee-based nonprofits, which include hospitals, nursing homes, health maintenance organizations, day-care centers, and summer camps.

"The critical question is whether the nonprofits in question provide the kind and quality of service that is unavailable from for-profit firms in the same industry," Hansmann testified in 1988.

"If they do not, then the case for tax exemption is quite nebulous. At most, it will simply produce a larger volume of services . . . and if this is what is desired, then we must ask why we do not extend the tax exemption to the for-profit firms as well."

One example of the kind of commercial nonprofit Hansmann is talking about is the Hazelden Foundation in Center City, Minnesota. Hazelden, best known as a drug and alcohol rehabilitation center, gets 95 percent of its funds from patient fees, publishing, and investments. Forty percent of Hazelden's $42 million in operating revenue in 1990 came from providing treatment. The other 60 percent came from its booming publishing business.

Hazelden officials say their publications are educational and an extension of therapy, and thus promote their exempt purpose. The group's 1990 IRS statement shows Hazelden paid no taxes on $25 million income from book and magazine sales. It paid self-help author Melody Beattie $1,123,389 in book royalties.

As large nonprofit organizations have matured, many have shed their traditional reliance on public contributions in favor of charging for their services.

In 1991, about three-quarters of the revenues reported to the IRS by large nonprofits came from selling services—such things as books and educational and health services. Public contributions, dues, and government grants accounted for the remaining one-quarter of their income.

"In effect, the nonprofits are growing in economic significance, and the way they are financing that growth is basically through nontraditional revenues from sales and services," Frank

Revenues of the Nonprofit Economy

Estimated
Annual
Revenues
$500 billion

Health Services 47%

Education/Research 21%

Religious Organizations 11%

Social/Legal Services 9%

Arts, Culture 3%
Civic, Social, Fraternal Organizations 3%
Foundations 2%
Other 4%

SOURCE: Industry and Inquirer Estimates   The Philadelphia Inquirer

Swain, chief counsel for the U.S. Small Business Administration, told a congressional committee in June 1988.

All but overlooked by mainstream economists, this reliance on fees and sales of services represents a fundamental shift in the nature of charities. And it raises important questions about how and whether these organizations are different from taxpaying businesses.

Consider Lankenau Hospital, a wealthy, debt-free institution in Wynnewood, outside Philadelphia. In 1979, contributions were nearly 16 percent of Lankenau's revenues. That year, gifts totaled $7,855,000 of the hospital's $50 million in revenues.

For the year ended June 30, 1990, Lankenau reported revenue of nearly $119 million. More than $102 million came from patient fees. Public contributions accounted for $998,000—less than 1 percent of all revenue.

Where did all the public contributions go? Did residents of Wynnewood suddenly stop supporting their local hospital? Not at all.

Lankenau set up a tax-exempt foundation in 1981 to bank its public contributions, which totaled $5.5 million in 1990. This had several effects. It established a separate organization to handle the hospital's substantial investment holdings. And it made the hospital appear less profitable.

For example, in 1990, Lankenau Hospital reported a profit of $7.5 million on revenues of nearly $119 million—a 6 percent profit margin. That was double the average profit of other area hospitals. Even so, it did not reflect the actual wealth of Lankenau because it did not include nearly $13 million earned by the Lankenau Foundation on its investments.

When the profits from the hospital and foundation are combined, Lankenau's 1990 profits total $20 million. And its profit margin increased to 15 percent on combined revenue of $135,318,000.

That same year, Lankenau Hospital Foundation accumulated more than three times as much in cash—$12.6 million—as it spent on charity and other services: $3.9 million. The $12.6 million was added to the Lankenau Hospital Foundation's already substantial investments, increasing its assets to $129 million. In 1991, those holdings increased to $137 million.

Lankenau had so much money banked in its foundation that, had it chosen, it could have cared for every patient that entered its doors in 1991 at no charge.

Lankenau spokesman Richard H. Wells said hospital trustees view the foundation's holdings as a "rainy day" fund and don't believe it would be good policy to use large amounts of the money to hold down costs. "If we were to use the resources of the foundation to pay these expenses, the foundation would dry up or disappear rather quickly. That would not serve the hospital or the community," Wells said.

Many large nonprofit organizations provide little charity today.

In 1990, the amount of free medical care given away by nonprofit hospitals averaged 6 percent of expenditures. Some inner-city hospitals provided substantially more, but some wealthy suburban hospitals spent as little as 1 percent on care for the poor.

The charitable outlays of private colleges and universities weren't much better. In 1990, they spent an average of just 7 percent of their own funds on student aid, a computer analysis of federal data of thirty-six hundred public and private nonprofit colleges shows.

Or consider private, tax-exempt foundations. Dominated by a few dozen huge institutions such as the Ford Foundation and the Pew Charitable Trusts, foundations controlled assets valued at $163 billion in 1991. On average they gave away about 5 percent of their wealth—the minimum required by law.

In the last three decades, the very definition of charity has become blurred. Federal, state, and local officials all use different—and sometimes conflicting—standards.

Since the 1960s, federal regulators have applied a broad definition of charity in overseeing nonprofits. Instead of requiring them to spend a substantial portion of their income on services to help the poor, Congress and the IRS have said that operating a hospital or school was sufficient justification alone for tax-exempt status.

Not everyone agreed with the broad definition. In 1985, the Supreme Court of Pennsylvania ruled that charities had to meet a tough, five-pronged test to justify tax exemption.

The requirements: advancing a charitable purpose; giving away a substantial portion of their services; benefiting a large number of poor or indigent persons; relieving the government of some burden; and operating free of a profit motive. Although these standards are more stringent, they are applied only if a tax agency challenges an exemption and the case lands in court.

In some cases, the conflicts between local and federal charity standards have resulted in organizations being declared profit-making businesses by regulators at one level and nonprofit by others. The prime example is Blue Cross and Blue Shield.

After determining they were not providing low-cost insurance, Congress revoked the tax exemption of the health plans in 1986 and started taxing them the next year. But in Pennsylvania, regulators still consider the state's five Blue Cross and Blue Shield plans tax-exempt. The state forgoes more than $150 million in tax revenues a year as a result.

The number of such discrepancies between state and federal standards is increasing. And the liberalization of charity rules may now be backfiring on federal regulators.

As more and more organizations qualify for tax-exempt status, government attorneys and revenue agents have been overwhelmed. For years, IRS attorneys have issued formal and informal rulings to nonprofit groups as a way of providing legal guidance in difficult areas. During the 1980s, the number of such rulings slowed dramatically because of staff shortages and increasing workloads.

"We are just not reaching our cases within the time frames that we have historically set as goals. That has been a major concern," Jeanne Gessay, chief of an IRS Rulings Branch, said in 1991. "Because of the budget, we were not permitted to hire for three years."

Many of the questions IRS attorneys confront today have to do with for-profit activities of nonprofits. Under the laissez-faire policies of the Reagan administration, nonprofits shifted billions of dollars into for-profit and not-for-profit businesses outside of their exempt purposes. And Congress and the IRS were caught flat-footed by the change.

In a speech, Owens of the IRS said: "I suspect the reason for . . . noncompliance is because tax advisers do not expect audit scrutiny of the organizations on whose behalf they file [tax] returns.

"Frankly, my comfort level is kind of low."

As for the nonprofits' comfort level, their profitability poses something of a public relations dilemma. They have developed their own special nomenclature. They don't call their earnings "profits"; they're "surpluses" or "excesses over expenditures."

The distinction was duly noted by the Erie County judge who heard the Hamot Medical Center tax case in 1990. Pointing out that Hamot had earned $57 million during the 1980s, Judge George Levin observed: "Hamot contends these funds are not profit but are revenue over expenses which are reinvested in operations. The evidence showed otherwise. Called profit or revenue over expenses, $57 million remained after expenses from 1981 to 1989. Hamot's revenue over expenses is profit, whether Hamot chooses to call it such or not."

Then the judge quoted from a famous scene in *Romeo and Juliet*, act 2, scene 2: "'What is in a name? That which we call a rose would by any other name smell as sweet.' Profit is profit, no matter where it is spent or what it is called. This level of profit is sweet by any name."

CHAPTER 2

For sale: Names of donors

Ever wonder why, when you give a donation to one charity, you're suddenly inundated with requests for money from other nonprofit groups? It's no accident.

All those heart-rending pleas to save the whales and feed the starving children are part of a massive high-tech campaign that charities use to solicit funds. A key element involves the buying and selling of donors' names—unbeknownst to the donors, but with the blessing of Congress—through a national network of middlemen-brokers.

Nonprofits refer to this practice as "renting" their mail lists. It generates tens of millions of dollars in fees each year and results in a hefty chunk of the twelve billion fund-raising letters mailed by nonprofits annually.

It works this way: Say you want to raise $1 million to fight a particular disease. All you have to do is call a broker who specializes in nonprofit groups. He can arrange a deal with another charity to rent its donor list. You then tap those donors for money.

Your cost? That depends on how many names you want and the financial profile of the donors. The wealthier and more generous the donors, the more valuable their names.

Generally, prices range from about $35 per one thousand

donor names to more than $100 per thousand, according to interviews and mail-list catalogs.

Want the list broken down by zip code? No problem. By size of donation? Again, no problem. Perhaps you want only the names of donors who've given in the last six months? That's no trouble, either.

For a modest fee, the list can be provided on computer tape. Mailing labels are available in a variety of preprinted forms. They run an extra dollar or so for every one thousand names.

The Philadelphia Inquirer examined more than one hundred mail-list transactions as part of its study of the $850 billion nonprofit economy. Typical was one involving the American Heart Association.

In September 1989, the Dallas-based nonprofit used an Armonk, New York, broker to buy a computerized mail list from Disabled American Veterans, one of the largest participants in the mail-list business. The list included names of all donors who had given at least $2 to the veterans group. Charge for the list: $82,528.81.

Charities say that if they didn't rent lists from time to time, their own donor lists would become outdated. After a time, they would be unable to raise sufficient funds to provide valuable services.

Disabled American Veterans, a congressionally chartered nonprofit organization with headquarters in Cold Spring, Kentucky, says the millions it has earned renting donors' names is critical to the services it provides 800,000 veterans. Court records and IRS filings show that the group earned more than $16 million between 1974 and 1985 providing donor names from its computerized list of six million donors.

In 1988 alone, the Disabled American Veterans processed 418 list requests, generating $1.8 million in fees. Of that, almost $300,000 went to brokers. Twice a year, the nonprofit publishes and distributes data cards listing its available donor groups and the charges for renting them.

Buying and selling donor lists comes at a price—the donor's privacy. Most donors have no idea their favorite charities sell their names and addresses to other groups. If donors object, it's up to them to make sure their names are removed from trading lists.

The federal government is of little help. Congress and regulators have adopted a series of contradictory policies about privacy rights of donors. The government prohibits nonprofits from disclosing the names of some donors in their public tax returns to protect the donors' privacy. But then the government allows charities to buy and sell names and addresses of these same donors to anyone who has the cash.

In December 1992, the Federal Communications Commission adopted rules prohibiting telemarketers from calling customers before 8 A.M. and after 9 P.M. Among the groups exempted from the new regulations: Charities and other nonprofits.

Asked the rationale for exempting nonprofits, a spokeswoman responded: "I know what the answer is going to be. They're going to say it would drive them all out of business."

The spokeswoman then chuckled and said: "Well, obviously there's been some lobbying going on."

Charities pay no taxes on most of the fees they earn from selling donor lists. The exception: when they sell their lists to profit-making firms. Then they must pay taxes. Such sales account for about 20 percent of all transactions.

Charities used to be required to pay taxes on all their income from list sales. In 1986, Congress amended the tax code as a result of lobbying from nonprofits to exempt income from sales to other nonprofits.

Congress adopted the change over the objections of the Internal Revenue Service and the Treasury Department, which contended that buying and selling donors' names was a commercial business.

It is a big business, too. In 1991, the Smithsonian Institution in Washington collected nearly $3.3 million from renting its mailing lists, and the National Audubon Society made $596,000. Three years earlier, the March of Dimes Birth Defects Foundation made $1.2 million renting its list.

For more than a decade, the IRS and the Disabled American Veterans have been involved in a legal dispute over income from donor lists. The IRS challenged the more than $16 million in donor-list fees that the Disabled American Veterans earned between 1974 and 1985. Initially, the United States Tax Court ruled that the fees were not taxable. But the Sixth Circuit Court of Appeals reversed that decision in July 1991. The legal dispute continues.

Other nonprofit groups have from time to time found themselves embroiled in struggles with the IRS over list rentals. In 1991, the IRS sent the Sierra Club a bill for $187,759 in back taxes for 1985 to 1987. Some of the bill was for income that the club earned by selling donor names and commissions from affinity credit card arrangements with its members. In an appeal filed with the United States Tax Court, Sierra Club attorneys argued that the income was not taxable.

A Delaware retailer brings in $17 million a year selling expensive strings of pearls, faux tortoise rattan tables, and other unusual gifts through twelve million catalogs mailed each year. The profit margin on goods sold is huge—sixty-five cents on every $1 taken in. If shoppers pay with credit cards, they can call a toll-free number seven days a week from 8 A.M. to midnight. Or they can visit one of the retailer's outlets just north of Wilmington, Delaware, or in Alexandria, Virginia.

What makes this retailer different from other trendy merchandisers? It is a nonprofit, tax-exempt museum. And it gets a break of up to $1 million a year on postage for its catalogs—subsidized by the United States government and, ultimately, taxpayers.

This is the Winterthur Museum and Garden, near Wilmington, Delaware, where revenue from the sale of merchandise is seventeen times the amount collected in admissions. Where two of the five highest-paid employees are the marketing director ($92,127 salary in 1991) and direct-mail director ($87,580 salary). Where officials have just begun to carefully consider whether the profit they make on merchandise sales should be taxed.

"We hadn't looked at it as closely until recently. Most things we sold we considered to be closely related to our [tax-exempt] mission," said Winterthur controller Richard F. Crozier.

In 1991, Winterthur had gross income of $11.2 million on $17.1 million in merchandise sales. For the first time ever, the museum reported $3.7 million as "unrelated business income" —income not covered by its tax exemption. After deducting expenses, the museum paid about $18,000 in federal income taxes.

In 1990 its gross profit on these sales was $8.8 million and in 1989 it was $9 million—all untaxed.

Museum or merchandiser? At times, it's tough to tell. Museums and other cultural institutions increasingly have gone commercial over the last decade as they try to raise money for their programs. The giant Metropolitan Museum of Art in New York now has a chain of thirteen retail outlets from California to Connecticut, many in malls. The museum also mails out millions of catalogs each year. In 1991, the Metropolitan Museum reported $45.5 million in gross profits on $87 million in merchandise and food sales. Those sales were nearly ten times what it collected in admissions. Out of all its revenues—$183 million—the museum declared $296,191 as "unrelated business income" and subject to federal income tax and paid $61,810 in tax.

When a museum opens a store outside the museum, for-profit competitors cry foul. "We feel the playing ground currently is not level," said William Edwards, vice-chairman of The Museum Company, which operates a national chain of thirty-two commercial stores that sell the same kinds of goods as museum shops.

Edwards doesn't object to museum stores at museums. But it's different when the museum opens a store in a mall. "They should be treated by the law like any private retailers that choose to open a store 1,000 miles from home," he said.

Edwards said that in at least five cases—two in Chicago and one each in Detroit, Atlanta, and Los Angeles—The Museum Company had a "handshake" agreement with a mall manager to rent space, then was bumped by a museum, which could pay higher rents because of its tax exemption. The museums' local social connections helped, too, Edwards said. "It never occurred to us that museums would take advantage of their tax exemptions," he said.

While some nonprofit museums compete with retailers, others are competing with for-profit movie theaters. In Philadelphia, the Franklin Institute opened its wraparound Tuttleman Omniverse Theater in 1990. Like other theaters in museums and aquariums, this 350-seat theater has shown educational science films, such as *Tropical Rainforest*. However, in 1992, between Thursday and Sunday nights, some shows were sold out. The movie was the *Rolling Stones at the Max*, which over seven months pulled in 30,498 people at $15 a ticket (including the option of also browsing the museum).

Cosponsored by classic rock radio station WYSP-FM in Philadelphia, the Stones movie opened in May 1992 with advertisements in the newspaper movie section touting: "See it larger than life on the four-story wraparound Omnimax screen with 56 speakers of floor-rattling digital sound!"

The Franklin Institute was by no means the only tax-exempt organization that made money from the Stones film. Museums and science centers across the nation showed the movie to boost evening attendance, said Susan Mander of Toronto-based Imax Corporation, the film's distributor. So far, more than a million people have seen it, accounting for $13 million in receipts.

The Franklin Institute did not consider the Rolling Stones movie commercial and is not declaring its receipts from the movie as unrelated business income, said spokeswoman Elaine Wilner. Some museum programs were built around the movie, she said, and people who attended were permitted to visit other museum exhibits.

Just less than half of the $450,000 gross went to Imax. The balance, about $237,000, went to the museum. Indeed, the museum sees all of what it does as program-related: In 1992, the Franklin Institute did not declare any of its $24 million in revenues, or $3.1 million in profit, subject to federal income taxes.

Cultural attractions are no small part of the economy. A 1989 study, which focused on twenty-eight cultural organizations in the Philadelphia area, found their annual ticket sales and admissions totaled $20 million. And audience spending on related activities, such as dining and parking, added up to another $33 million, according to the study sponsored by the Pew Charitable Trusts in Philadelphia.

But looking at revenues only from admissions understates the size of the cultural sector. For example, the four museums near Philadelphia's Benjamin Franklin Parkway—the Philadelphia Museum of Art (admission: $6), the Franklin Institute ($9.50), the Academy of Natural Sciences ($6), and the Please Touch Museum ($5)—had total revenues of $68 million in 1990. The figure includes admissions, merchandising, donations, grants, dividends, and interest.

Nevertheless, museum fees have been rising: To take a family of four—two children and two adults—to the Franklin Institute for the combination package of museum, Omniverse Theater, and planetarium costs $54. And that's without the hot dogs.

When it comes to special-interest politics, nonprofit groups play the game as well as anyone. And they do it the old-fashioned way: with money, especially PAC money.

Take the National Cattlemen's Association, a tax-exempt trade group for ranchers, based in Englewood, Colorado. It is one of hundreds of nonprofit groups that lobby Congress every year. You thought nonprofit organizations weren't allowed to politick? Wrong.

Under the tax code and election laws, only charities—not other nonprofits—are prohibited from participating in political activities. But even charities can set up separate nonprofit organizations under a different section of the tax code to lobby Congress and form political action committees.

The cattlemen figured out years ago how to play the game. Their nonprofit association divides its efforts among lobbying, promotion, and professional activities. Like other trade groups, it spends heavily to gain access to lawmakers, particularly those who regulate the cattlemen's business.

Between May 1987 and February 1990, the Cattlemen's Association distributed honoraria and speaking fees totaling $16,000 to sixteen members of Congress, thirteen of whom sat on key agriculture and interior committees, campaign finance records show. Between January 1989 and June 1992, the cattlemen's PAC contributed $564,104 to Washington legislators. Contributions were tilted toward members of agriculture committees.

What do ranchers want from Congress? For starters, there's the federal lands grazing program, a taxpayer-subsidized arrangement in which livestock owners get to graze their cattle on government lands at very cheap rates.

In 1991, the Bureau of Land Management awarded more than thirty thousand grazing permits. Ranchers paid $1.97 a month for each head of cattle—about one-fourth the grazing charge for private land.

According to the General Accounting Office, a relatively small group of wealthy investors and big corporations controls nearly half of the public lands under permit. A June 1992 report by the congressional agency said that five hundred individuals and corporations—or about 2 percent of all permit-holders—controlled seventy-six million acres of public rangelands. Among the select five hundred: Metropolitan Life Insurance Company,

Sierra Pacific Resources, Pacific Power & Light, Texaco, and a number of millionaire rancher-investors.

"It's outrageous that the American taxpayer is forced to subsidize millionaires like Laurence Rockefeller and huge corporations like Metropolitan Life and Getty," Representative Mike Synar, Democrat from Oklahoma, said after the GAO report was released. Synar estimates that the government could be getting an additional $75 million to $100 million annually. But his repeated attempts to raise grazing fees to market levels "to give federal welfare cowboys a good dose of free enterprise" have not been supported by his congressional colleagues. Ranchers and their lobbying associations say the fees are appropriate and take into account some hidden costs, including the expense of maintaining the property.

In all, more than one thousand nonprofit groups have set up tax-exempt networks to lobby for their special interests. They include a broad range of business, advocacy, and political groups. Usually, they are lobbying for federal bounty. For example:

- WHEATPAC, the political action committee of the nonprofit National Association of Wheat Growers, contributed $120,000 to members of Congress between September 1988 and June 1992, with half going to key agriculture committee members. Federal subsidies for wheat growers totaled nearly $3 billion in 1991.
- The National Cotton Council distributed $21,000 in honoraria to twelve members of the House Agriculture Committee between December 1986 and September 1990. One legislator, Jerry Huckaby, Democratic representative from Louisiana, received $9,000. Huckaby is chairman of the Agriculture Subcommittee on Cotton, Rice and Sugar. The council's Political Action Committee for the Advancement of Cotton contributed $498,538 to campaigns of federal lawmakers between November 1988 and June 1992, much of it to key agriculture committee members. Federal subsidies for cotton growers totaled $382 million in 1991 and an estimated $1.3 billion in 1992, according to the United States Agriculture Department.
- The American Sugarbeet Growers Association, a nonprofit trade group, awarded $14,000 in honoraria and speaking fees to members of Congress between 1988 and 1992 and

another $795,140 in campaign contributions through its PAC. A federal quota system that limits the importation of cheaper foreign sugar results in artificially high prices for domestic sugar.

Spokespersons for these and other nonprofit trade and advocacy groups say they simply are trying to establish a political presence. And one way you do that is with money.

"Whether it's the AMA, the Tobacco Institute, the National Association of Realtors, or the Teamsters, you want to be part of the political process," said Walker Merryman, vice-president of the tax-exempt Tobacco Institute. "It doesn't guarantee you anything. But it ensures that members of Congress and our groups can meet and talk about issues that have a direct bearing on us."

Needless to say, the overwhelming majority of individual taxpayers don't have this level of access—even though they are indirectly underwriting the lobbying efforts of special interest groups. Nor do they enjoy the tax breaks these groups get.

The Tobacco Institute is a good example of how an industry gains access. Between June 1986 and December 1990, it gave out $537,676 in speaking fees to more than one hundred members of Congress, including most of the House Agriculture Subcommittee on Tobacco and Peanuts. North Carolina Democrat Charles G. Rose, subcommittee chairman, received $10,000 in five separate $2,000 payments.

"We invited members of Congress to speak to groups of tobacco industry executives in Washington and also at our annual legislative conference," Merryman said. "Most of the time, members would speak about issues that had a direct bearing on us— taxes, advertising, that sort of thing. They might comment on pending legislation or legislative trends they knew about that might affect us."

In 1989, House members agreed to a ban on speaking fees, effective in January 1991, in exchange for a hefty salary increase. That hasn't stopped legislators from accepting trips to Bermuda, Florida, and California paid for by tax-exempt special interest groups.

Another tax-exempt group that invests heavily in lobbying and PAC contributions is the American Medical Association. Between 1981 and 1992, the doctors' group handed out more than $12 million—twice as much as the next highest health PAC.

During the 1980s, Congress began to look at ways to control rising federal reimbursements to physicians, which have increased an average of 13 percent a year since 1965. They now exceed $26 billion a year.

Medical PAC contributions have increased as Congress has taken up the issue of national health reform. The nonprofit group Common Cause reported that the health-care industry contributed more than $60 million to congressional candidates during the 1980s. Current members received $43 million of that.

CHAPTER 3

Charitable hospitals: Where's the charity?

Graduate Hospital once was a struggling community hospital in South Philadelphia with a clear-cut mission: to care for the poor and help train doctors. Most of its beds were occupied by patients who couldn't pay. In recognition of its charity, Graduate was exempted from paying taxes.

More than a century later, Philadelphians still subsidize the hospital through their taxes. But the similarity ends there.

Today, Graduate Hospital is part of a sprawling $400 million health-care conglomerate that includes seven hospitals, a profit-making HMO, dozens of subsidiaries, fifty-three hundred employees, a well-paid executive staff, and lavish headquarters in a renovated Gothic church.

Donations, once a hospital mainstay, account for less than 1 percent of Graduate's revenue now. Most of its money comes from fees the hospital charges, just like any commercial business. And there is relatively little charity. Less than 3 percent of its $120 million budget in 1990 went to providing free medical treatment.

Graduate is not unique. It is a case history of how hundreds of nonprofit hospitals across America, using their tax subsidies, have been transformed from small charitable institutions into modern medical empires—at a cost of more than $8 billion a

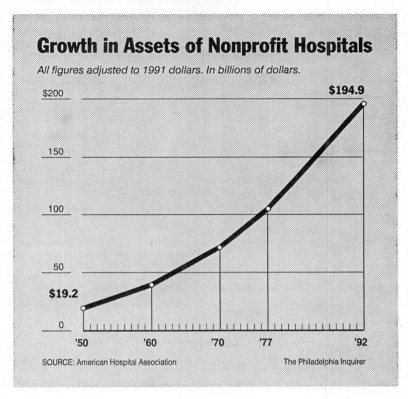

Growth in Assets of Nonprofit Hospitals

All figures adjusted to 1991 dollars. In billions of dollars.

$200

$194.9

150

100

50

$19.2

0

'50　　　'60　　　'70　'77　　　　'92

SOURCE: American Hospital Association　　　The Philadelphia Inquirer

year in lost federal and state taxes. That tax subsidy, plus others, has spurred the phenomenal growth in nonprofit hospitals. As a group, they tripled in size during the 1980s.

Hospitals now are the single largest segment of the $850 billion tax-free economy, accounting for nearly one-quarter of all assets. Since 1950, their assets have grown tenfold, from $19 billion to $195 billion, after adjusting for inflation.

Because they pay no taxes, many hospitals have accumulated huge profits and used them to build new hospital wings, to buy expensive equipment, and to diversify into other businesses. That has led to overbuilding and overstaffing of hospitals and has helped push health-care costs out of sight. On any given night, one-third of all hospital beds in America are empty.

In the last two decades, the average cost of a hospital stay has gone from $615 in 1970 to $1,900 in 1980 to $5,000 in

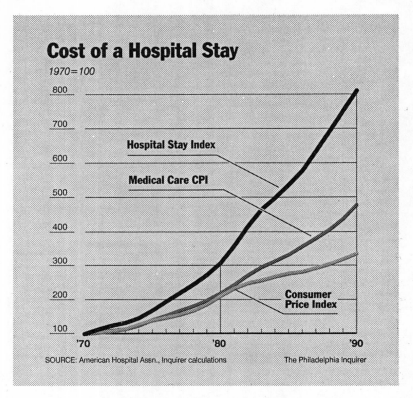

Cost of a Hospital Stay
1970=100

Hospital Stay Index

Medical Care CPI

Consumer Price Index

'70   '80   '90

SOURCE: American Hospital Assn., Inquirer calculations   The Philadelphia Inquirer

1990—a rise of 713 percent. That was three times the rate of inflation. In the same period, the revenue of nonprofit hospitals increased from about $14 billion to more than $150 billion, or four times the rate of inflation.

Despite nonprofit hospitals' tax-exempt status, their charges to patients are no lower than those at for-profit hospitals. And charity care, once the reason for these hospitals' privileged tax-exempt status, has declined. It now accounts for about 6 percent of hospital expenditures nationwide—3 percent in metropolitan Philadelphia.

Today, the government—or, more precisely, taxpayers—have taken over much of the charity function through such programs as Medicaid and Medicare, which have pumped more than $660 billion into nonprofit hospitals since 1965.

Nevertheless, the hospitals kept the tax exemption they had been granted for providing free care.

Sound too good to be true? It gets even better.

Tax-exempt hospitals no longer *have* to provide charity care. If an uninsured worker or homeless person needs elective surgery, yet has no money, the hospital may turn away the patient without fear of losing its tax-exempt status. That has been the government's official policy since 1969, when the IRS changed its definition of charity, in part as a result of extensive hospital lobbying.

Today, many nonprofit hospitals have accumulated huge surpluses. Most of this money has gone to grow the business.

Consider some findings from *The Inquirer's* eighteen-month examination of nonprofits:

- Hospitals have moved more than $3 billion into tax-exempt foundations and holding companies, where they have financed acquisitions, paid big salaries, and underwritten investments in for-profit businesses. One effect of these transfers is to make the hospitals appear less wealthy than they really are. Officials say the funds are used to buy equipment and replace old buildings. But little seems to flow back to the hospitals. In 1990, hospital foundations in Pennsylvania plowed back just 5 percent of their money, an analysis of tax returns of fifty-two hospital foundations shows. Thirty-nine percent of the money went for foundations' administrative overhead and salaries; 56 percent went into stocks, bonds, and certificates of deposit.

- More than $40 billion was used to build hospital towers, offices, and parking garages. At the time of this expansion, the 1980s, hospital use was declining by 13 percent. Patients are paying for this overbuilding: Between 1984 and 1988, the portion of patient bills that covers hospital capital costs increased on average from $313 to $523.

- Billions of dollars were used to expand hospitals' corporate networks. Lutheran General Health Care System, a $600 million conglomerate near Chicago, diversified widely in the 1980s, operating sixty-five subsidiaries, including a nationwide chain of drug and alcohol rehabilitation centers. This aggressive strategy later backfired, forcing officials to reduce the value of their holdings by $103 million.

- At least $1 billion has been invested in commercial spinoffs. Examples from the 250 hospital IRS forms that *The Inquirer* examined include auto-leasing companies, book publishers, hotels, laundries, pharmacies, restaurants, parking lots, travel agencies, a duck hunting lodge, and, in the case of the Mayo Clinic, an airport management company.

Why would a hospital invest in an airport? "The Mayo Clinic has patients come from all over the world. To make sure they could get here, we had to have an airport," said Chris Gade, a spokesman for the medical facility in Rochester, Minnesota.

As nonprofit hospitals have moved further afield, competitors and taxing agencies have become concerned. In Allentown, Pennsylvania, a health conglomerate diversified so widely in the 1980s that it drew the attention of local tax assessors and a county judge. HealthEast had invested $5 million of hospital profits in thirteen commercial businesses.

HealthEast owned a pharmacy, a telephone paging service, a medical equipment business, real estate developments, a walk-in surgical center, medical office buildings, a weight-loss program, an employee benefits business, a computer information service, at least three private medical practices, and a television production company.

"The conventional wisdom during the '80s was . . . by being competitive and using competitive economic principles, you would in effect drive down the cost of health care," said Vaughn Gower, chief financial officer. "For the first time, nonprofits even allowed thinking to creep in they could be involved in for-profit activities."

In 1988, Lehigh County Orphans' Court judge Robert K. Young decided to do an accounting of "the stewardship" of the conglomerate. Young's study lasted more than a year. In a report in July 1990, he concluded: "The problem which must be addressed by the HealthEast Board of Trustees is a prevailing perception, unfortunately true in some respects, that HealthEast is misusing its power."

Young wrote: "If those in charge of hospitals have of late become too concerned with operating a business, as opposed to administering a charity, steps must be taken by the trustees to place the hospital back on the proper track. In short, . . . hospitals should concentrate on providing quality health care at affordable rates, and not be overly concerned with turning a profit."

Since the judge's report, HealthEast has shed at least eight of the for-profit businesses, and also its name. The nonprofit business is now called Lehigh Valley Health Network.

Belatedly, the Internal Revenue Service has begun to look more closely at the diversification, too. "There's no question, hospitals are a good example of how some large nonprofits have changed, becoming businesslike, even investing in for-profit ventures. They present one of the most challenging areas for us," said Marcus S. Owens, director of the IRS's Exempt Organizations Technical Division.

In 1991, the IRS announced it was changing the way it audits nonprofit hospitals to take into account their increasing complexity and commercial nature. Since then, the agency has begun twenty-three comprehensive audits. "I expect, based on the information to date, that we will see some revocations" of hospitals' tax-exempt status, Owens said.

When charity patients arrived at the hospital at Eighteenth and Lombard streets in Philadelphia a century ago, it was called The Polyclinic Hospital. By the early 1920s, it had become the clinical training facility for the University of Pennsylvania's new Graduate School of Medicine, called Graduate Hospital. But the modern history of the 103-year-old hospital begins in 1977, when the University of Pennsylvania decided to spin off Graduate as a separate corporation. Enter Harold Cramer, a Philadelphia lawyer specializing in health care, and a small group of associates.

Under its new leadership, Graduate obtained $38 million in tax-exempt bonds to build a new patient-care tower. Its revenues increased. And for the first time in years, it showed a profit. In fact, after recording a loss of $676,815 in 1980, Graduate posted profits in each of the next 11 years. They totaled $47 million.

The profits helped underwrite a rapid expansion in the 1980s. Among dozens of subsidiaries that Graduate created were:

- X-RAY Associates, a commercial radiology business incorporated in August 1984.
- Graduate Surgi-Centers, a for-profit walk-in surgical center incorporated in October 1984.
- Graduate Rehabilitation Services, a for-profit physical-therapy service incorporated in May 1986.
- Lombard Laboratory, a for-profit joint venture with Smith-Kline Bio-Science Laboratories incorporated in July 1986.

- Mt. Sinai Radiology, a for-profit company incorporated in February 1988 to provide radiology services.
- Graduate Health System, a nonprofit management firm set up in 1988 to oversee the expanding network. It is the parent company of Graduate Hospital and its spinoff businesses.
- U/G Holding Corporation, a nonprofit firm incorporated in the late 1980s to pay key executives of Graduate Health System. These salaries totaled $1.5 million in 1990, including Cramer's $350,749.

Another $4 million was used to buy and renovate a 112-year-old English Gothic church at Twenty-second and Chestnut streets —now corporate headquarters for Graduate Health System. The award-winning building features a great hammerbeam roof, sixty-five-foot glass wall overlooking an atrium, cherry wood-paneled rooms, and a gas fireplace in the executive offices.

Cramer, chairman and chief executive, said that purchasing and renovating the church was cheaper than leasing office space. Still, he declined to be photographed there because of concern that outsiders might look at the church "as a Taj Mahal."

Graduate's expanding network also included medical office buildings, parking lots, a sports medicine center, an occupational therapy clinic, a limited partnership to develop products for cosmetic surgery, a for-profit cholesterol control center, and a for-profit company to develop new medical equipment.

Tax returns and financial records show Graduate had at least thirty-five corporations and partnerships under its corporate umbrella as of April 1991. Twenty-one were profit-making businesses, which are subject to corporate income taxes. Some were later abandoned.

In the late 1980s, Graduate also began to buy other hospitals and health-care providers. In 1987, as part of a noncash merger, Graduate acquired Zurbrugg Health Foundation, which operates medical centers in Riverside and Willingboro, New Jersey. In 1988, Graduate paid $11.2 million for Mt. Sinai Hospital, a financially ailing facility at Fifth and Reed streets in South Philadelphia owned by the Albert Einstein Healthcare Foundation. A year later, Graduate purchased John Hancock HealthPlans, a for-profit HMO with about forty thousand members. It paid $1.8 million in cash, assumed liabilities of $11.8 million, and agreed to pay another $1.7 million that the health plan owed to another company. The HMO was renamed Greater Atlantic Health Plan.

In a related transaction, Graduate bought Philadelphia Health Associates, a for-profit corporation that provides physician services to the HMO. It cost more than $3.6 million, including liabilities of $2.1 million. Graduate officials guaranteed payment of an $8.4 million mortgage on a medical office property as part of the transaction. In 1991, Graduate acquired Community General Hospital in Reading in a noncash merger, with the 164-bed facility becoming a subsidiary of Graduate Health System. And in 1993, Graduate bought two hospitals from Osteopathic Medical Center of Philadelphia for $16 million, plus a $12 million note. The $16 million came from a refinancing of tax-exempt bonds.

Cramer, sixty-five, said the many acquisitions and subsidiaries were part of a master plan to build a regional health-care network. "That's what I have been trying to put together. We want to have a vertically integrated health-care system because we think this will allow us to provide health care for significantly lower costs than anyone else."

Under this plan, patients with less severe problems will be treated at Graduate's lower-cost suburban hospitals, while more involved cases will be referred to the more costly Graduate Hospital. Greater Atlantic complements this strategy because it gives Graduate another source of referrals. And Graduate's many for-profit and nonprofit subsidiaries allow it to provide patients the equivalent of one-stop shopping, Cramer said.

"It's a big business, a very big complicated business," Cramer said. "But if you don't run it like a business, you won't be around to service the community."

Patients, government, and private insurers are paying for Graduate's remarkable growth. Graduate is one of the most expensive hospitals in the city, according to industry data. Between 1987 and 1991, patient revenues increased an average of 13 percent a year. That was more than twice the inflation rate.

A majority of the hospital's patients have private insurance or pay cash. The rest—42 percent—are covered by Medicare and Medicaid, the taxpayer-financed programs for the elderly and poor. In 1991, Graduate's payments from the government under these programs totaled $62 million.

Taxpayers also have helped underwrite the bulk of its expansion and acquisitions. At least $56 million from the sale of tax-exempt bonds has been used to buy hospitals or pay back Grad-

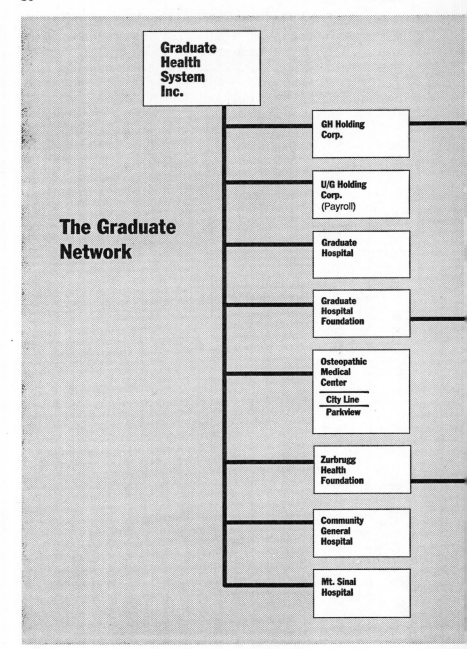

Graduate
Health
System
Inc.

The Graduate
Network

GH Holding
Corp.

U/G Holding
Corp.
(Payroll)

Graduate
Hospital

Graduate
Hospital
Foundation

Osteopathic
Medical
Center
City Line
Parkview

Zurbrugg
Health
Foundation

Community
General
Hospital

Mt. Sinai
Hospital

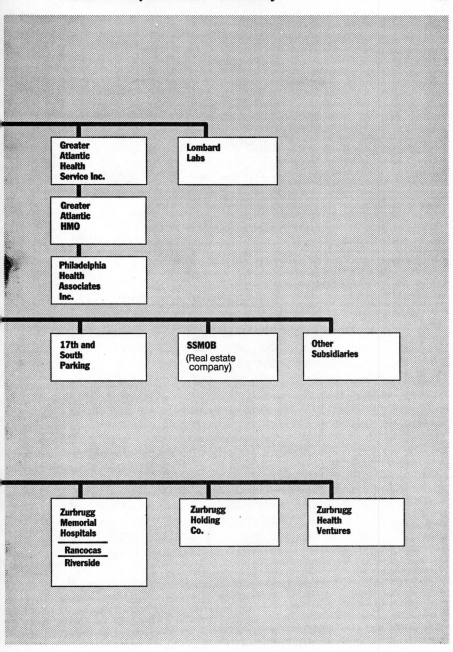

uate for loans and operating losses. Another $59 million in tax-exempt bonds has gone to fund equipment, buildings, and parking garages.

Among the many moves Graduate has funded with tax-exempt bonds was its acquisition of Mt. Sinai Hospital. Taxpayers have subsidized this transaction in several ways.

Initially, Graduate officials used an $11.2 million bank loan to purchase the 203-bed acute-care hospital. Later in 1988, they refinanced the loan with $20.2 million in tax-exempt bonds issued by the Philadelphia Hospitals Authority. At the time, Graduate officials planned to continue operating Mt. Sinai as a community hospital, even though it had lost $13.2 million in 1987.

"Strategically, what it would do is give us a community hospital," Cramer said. "It occurred at the same time my crystal ball said we should be developing a regional health-care network." It was, Cramer acknowledges, "very risky. The losses were much bigger than we knew."

Between February 1988 and June 1991, Mt. Sinai lost nearly $32 million, according to tax returns and financial records. In 1990 alone, it lost $16.8 million. To keep the hospital afloat, Graduate officials advanced Mt. Sinai $20 million, with most of it coming from Graduate Hospital.

In May 1989, Cramer resigned as a senior partner of Mesirov, Gelman, Jaffe, Cramer & Jamieson, his longtime law firm, to become chief executive officer of Graduate Health System. He had been its board chairman.

"The board [of Graduate Health System] asked me to do it. The Mt. Sinai situation was killing us," he said.

Graduate officials soon decided to stop operating Mt. Sinai as a community hospital. In a series of steps, they shut its emergency room, stopped doing general surgery, and ended routine services. Later, they marketed the hospital as a specialty center for cosmetic surgery, drug and alcohol detoxification, rehabilitation services, and psychiatric services—in effect, a boutique medical center.

A key strategy behind these moves was to attract more private-paying patients, and to maximize reimbursements from Medicare and Medicaid. The way to do this, Graduate officials decided, was to offer services that are not subject to the government's stringent payment systems. Unlike most services, the government pays hospitals their full costs on detox, rehab, and psychiatric services.

The Mt. Sinai strategy was outlined in a December 1991 document submitted to the Hospitals Authority of Philadelphia. "Mt. Sinai has an increased percentage of cost-based payers over the prior years," the document reads. "The majority [50–60 percent] of in-patient acute care and skilled nursing beds are currently exempt from the prospective payment system, resulting in decreases in bad debt and free care and other administrative adjustments."

The keys to the new Mt. Sinai strategy were to "limit competition with neighboring facilities; de-emphasize location through specialized product lines and regionalize the referral base," the document says.

The approach apparently worked. In 1991, Mt. Sinai reduced its operating loss to about $800,000. And in 1992, the revamped hospital made a $37,000 profit, Cramer said.

How does this strategy jibe with Mt. Sinai's status as a charitable, tax-exempt community hospital? "There's a real need for these services. Our adolescent psych and geriatric rehab programs are full. And we've added a skilled nursing facility, which is also in great demand," Cramer said.

As for charity, Cramer said Mt. Sinai and Graduate System's other hospitals "never turn anyone away. We take everyone who shows up . . . including AIDS patients who other hospitals send us by cab."

For taxpayers, the Mt. Sinai saga doesn't end here. In late 1991, Graduate sold $112 million in tax-exempt bonds through the Hospitals Authority of Philadelphia as part of a systemwide refinancing. According to an offering statement, bond proceeds were to be used to refinance earlier debts; fund various capital projects, including an underground garage; and pay back Graduate Hospital and Graduate Health System the $20 million they had advanced Mt. Sinai to keep it afloat.

Ordinarily, tax-exempt bonds are used to pay for new hospital construction, not to insulate a hospital from the consequences of an investment gone bad. Yet, in this instance, that is what took place. Graduate officials were able to recoup a substantial portion of their operating losses at Mt. Sinai—and to do it with the help of the public, whose taxes make up for the interest lost on tax-exempt bonds.

Cramer said using tax-exempt bonds to pay back Graduate is not unusual. "Federal policy allows for it. This is not something that was created for Graduate," he said. "This is not something I'm borrowing and am not able to pay back."

In essence, the risky Mt. Sinai purchase became a risk-free venture—thanks to taxpayers.

For years, hospitals earned their tax exemption by giving away a substantial amount of care.

Until 1969, they were required to provide free medical care to the extent of their financial resources—what was known as the "financial ability" standard. It reflected the long-held position of the government that charity should benefit the poor, not an indefinite class of people.

In 1969, IRS officials dropped the financial ability standard in favor of a "community service" standard, which defined charity in broader terms. Hospitals now qualified as tax-exempt charities because they promoted health services for their communities.

"Like the relief of poverty and the advancement of education and religion, [the provision of health care by hospitals] is one of the purposes in the general law of charity that is deemed beneficial to the community as a whole, even though the class of beneficiaries eligible to receive a direct benefit from its activities does not include all members of the community, such as indigent members of the community," the IRS ruled. In other words, just being there is enough—whether poor people are helped or not.

Nonprofit hospitals had been lobbying for such a change for years. In discussions with IRS officials and testimony before congressional panels, hospital officials contended that most Americans had government or private health coverage. There just weren't that many charity cases, they said.

In 1968, Congress appeared to be on the threshold of passing legislation adopting the hospitals' point of view. But differences between House and Senate committees over an acceptable definition of charity proved irreconcilable, and the issue was dropped.

Enter the IRS. The tax agency also had been studying the issue and interviewing hospital administrators. Rather than wait for Congress to pass a law, the IRS rewrote its own regulations, loosening its definition of charity.

"They accepted the hospital industry's point of view that there was no more charity problem," said Daniel C. Schaffer, a professor of tax law at Northeastern University. "On the basis of their representations, the service decided to discharge hospitals of their responsibilities."

Schaffer said IRS attorneys believed that Medicaid would cover most uninsured and indigent Americans. Again, that's what the hospitals had said.

In fact, Medicaid never came close to covering all of the nation's poor. Congress left it up to individual states to set the financial eligibility criteria. Most states set them so stringently that the standards excluded many of the poor. Today, twenty-eight years after Medicaid's enactment, the program covers fewer than half—49 percent, in fact—of the estimated thirty-two million Americans living below the poverty level.

Despite such glaring holes in the nation's health-care safety net, the IRS did not revisit its 1969 charity decision until Congress raised the issue in 1991. Even then, Michael J. Graetz, an assistant secretary of the Treasury, said there was no reason to change.

"A community benefit standard reflects the longstanding proposition that the promotion of health is a charitable purpose and recognizes the potential for a variety of means of fulfilling that purpose," he told the House Ways and Means Committee in 1991.

In an interview, Schaffer was more blunt: "The IRS has basically been in denial for the last quarter-century. It's as though they turned their heads so they wouldn't see what was happening. It's disgraceful."

Congress did not hold follow-up hearings on the IRS's 1969 decision. Nor did it examine the link between charity care and the tax breaks awarded nonprofit hospitals until Representative Brian J. Donnelly (Democrat from Massachusetts) and Representative Edward R. Roybal (Democrat from California) introduced bills to tighten charity care standards in 1991. Neither proposal advanced past the committee stage.

"It's very difficult politically to raise these issues. Hospitals are very powerful and have an array of lobbyists," said Donnelly, who retired in January 1993 after sixteen years in Washington. "You don't get any votes for taking on the hospitals."

"Congress was asleep on this issue," said Daniel M. Fox,

president of the nonprofit Milbank Memorial Fund and a col-
league of Schaffer's. "It allowed the IRS to set both tax and
health policy and then provided no oversight. For the last twenty
years, hospitals have essentially had a free ride."

I t has been a great ride, unmatched by all but a handful of
other industries.

At a time when many businesses have been in retreat, shut-
ting plants and laying off workers, the hospital industry booms:
- Hospital employment more than doubled nationally, from
1.8 million workers to 3.7 million, in the last two decades—
making it one of the economy's most dynamic performers.
- Hospital wages more than tripled between 1977 and 1990—
to $70 billion. That was double the general rate of inflation.
And those rising wages are one of the key factors in higher
health costs.

The number of Americans reporting income between $30,000
and $40,000 rose 48 percent in the 1980s. The number of non-
profit hospital employees reporting income over $30,000 rose
ten times as fast.

At specific hospitals, such as these in Philadelphia, the growth
was more dazzling: At Thomas Jefferson University, the number
increased from 295 to 3,307 employees; at Pennsylvania Hospital, it increased from 57 to 1,027; at Children's Hospital, the
number swelled from 21 to 694; at Graduate Hospital, it rose
from 24 to 657.

"Hospitals are the new steel mills of the '90s," said Tom
Chakurda, spokesman for Allegheny General Hospital, which
runs five hospitals in Philadelphia. "Officials sometimes over-
look that when they go looking for hospitals to pay taxes."

The reason for such dramatic increases lies in the changing
nature of hospitals. With the adoption of ever-more complicated
technology, their need for more highly skilled workers has grown.

Today, more than 65 percent of nurses in hospitals are regis-
tered nurses, who typically earn between $35,000 and $65,000.
That's up from 49 percent a decade ago.

Increased demand for therapists and technicians also has
pushed up salaries. And salaries of hospital administrators now
often exceed executive pay at comparable-sized companies.

All of this—spurred by the enormous growth of tax-exempt

Growth of 5 Philadelphia-area Hospitals
Not adjusted for inflation.

Hospital	Revenues In millions		Profits (Losses) In millions		Net assets In millions		Number of employees earning $30,000 or more	
	1980	1991	1980	1991	1980	1991	1980	1991
Children's Hospital of Philadelphia	$57	$296	$2.0	$16	$66	$113	21	1,041
Graduate Hospital	45	164	(0.7)	7	10	70	24	734
Hahnemann University*†	153	619	6.0	9	87	137	271	1,736
Lankenau Hospital	52	131	6.0	8	73	119	6	844
Thomas Jefferson University*	165	568	5.0	16	124	387	295	3,357

* Includes medical and graduate schools
† Figures for 1981; 1980 figures not available

SOURCE: Hospital tax returns   The Philadelphia Inquirer

hospitals—has helped drive up prices. It is the health-care monster that the government is trying to wrestle to the ground.

In a report issued in January 1993, the United States Commerce Department cited the labor intensity of the health-care industry and the high earnings for professional, administrative, and technical workers as the most important reason medical expenditures increased by 11.5 percent in 1992 to $838 billion.

Perry J. Leon, sixty-four, of Northeast Philadelphia has strong views about such costs. In November 1991, Leon was charged $6,373.50 for an operation to remove a cataract in one eye. The outpatient procedure at Rolling Hill Hospital lasted "about one hour," Leon said. Including recovery time, he spent five hours at the hospital.

Leon's insurer, Travelers Insurance Company, paid the hospital $5,576.50. The hospital billed Leon for the balance. He re-fuses to pay.

"The hospitals are committing a crime against the sick, and this has an effect on the nation's economy, on working people and unions," Leon said. "I'm lucky. I have insurance through work. But lots of people don't.

"How a one-hour procedure on one eye can cost so much is fantasy. That's what I told them. I said, 'This is a fantasy. I am not going to pay. If you want to go to court, let's go.' It's been more than a year and I haven't heard from them," he said.

Hospital officials say criticism like Leon's is unfair. Yes, their costs are high, but that's because of the sophisticated pro-cedures and elaborate technology. Instead of criticizing, pa-tients and politicians ought to be thankful for the important role hospitals play in the economy, they say.

"One in every eight workers in the [Philadelphia region] owes his or her job to hospitals," the Delaware Valley Hospital Council said in 1992. Citing a $40,000 study paid for by the council, it said hospitals contribute more than $5.5 billion a year to the economy.

"Hospitals are to the Delaware Valley what cars are to De-troit," said Hospital Council president Jeff Flood.

Indeed, hospitals are an important economic force in the region. But their tax breaks are based on their charitable com-munity service, not the jobs they provide. And the profits that some have accumulated make it hard to argue persuasively that they are trying to control costs.

Consider these examples from tax filings with the IRS for the years 1989 through 1991:

- The Mayo Foundation in Rochester, Minnesota, owned $531 million in stocks, bonds, and securities and controlled prop-erty worth $773 million. In 1986 and 1987, Mayo accommo-dated patients who were retiring to warmer climates by building a $27 million clinic near Jacksonville, Florida, and another $65 million facility in Scottsdale, Arizona.
- The Cleveland Clinic Foundation held $207 million in cash and investments, plus property worth $627 million. Clinic officials opened a $150 million satellite facility in Fort Lau-derdale in 1987. They, too, said they were following their patients south.
- The Methodist Hospital System in Houston held invest-

ments worth $600 million and property valued at $408 million. Among its many investments: the Chez Eddy, a self-described "highly acclaimed gourmet restaurant," and a duck lodge, since sold. Between 1986 and 1990, its diversified holdings generated $100 million, yet only $3 million was returned to the hospital. Meanwhile, the hospital's prices rose an average of 7 percent a year.

- Thomas Jefferson University in Philadelphia had investments worth $247 million, and owned property and equipment worth nearly $356 million.
- Main Line Health System, which includes Bryn Mawr, Lankenau, and Paoli Hospitals in suburban Philadelphia, plus twenty-one other affiliates, held $230 million in investments and $411 million in property.
- Children's Hospital of Philadelphia and its affiliates owned nearly $190 million in stocks, bonds, and other investments, plus $175 million in property and equipment.

Like other hospitals, Children's has used its surplus to expand rather than hold the line on patient charges. Those keep going up, averaging 7 percent a year for the last five years. Says Children's president Edmond Notebaert, "Our increases have been lower than those of other comparable hospitals."

In 1989, Children's opened a $48 million building for outpatient care and administration. In 1992, the hospital sold about $200 million in tax-exempt bonds to renovate Children's Hospital and build a $117-million research center and parking garage.

The hospital said it would contribute $69 million. Patients and taxpayers will pay for the rest in at least five ways: Patients will pay higher charges to help cover increased overhead and debt; federal tax dollars will underwrite much of the medical research; investors who buy the hospital's tax-exempt bonds will receive tax breaks, resulting in a loss to the Treasury; a low-interest $9 million loan from the state will help pay for the project; and the new research facility will be off the city's property tax rolls, which means the public will shoulder a larger share of the tax burden.

How much charity care do nonprofit hospitals provide? Does it equal the value of their $8 billion tax exemption? The American Hospital Association says that hospitals provided $8.9 billion worth of free treatment in 1989. "The problem is one in which we are seeing the indigent and the uninsured patients that are showing up at our hospitals at a greater and greater number, with nowhere to shift that cost," Jack W. Owen, acting president of the American Hospital Association, told Congress in July 1991.

But some critics say the hospitals' figures are inflated, because they include bad debt and other costs that are not charity. "The hospitals are playing with the numbers, and in some cases their charity care doesn't come close to the value of their exemption," said Donnelly, the former congressman.

A 1990 study of nonprofit hospitals in five states by the General Accounting Office showed that 57 percent provided less charity care than the tax benefits they derived. Overall, industry data show charity care accounts for about 6 percent of nonprofit hospitals' budgets. In Pennsylvania, the average is about 3 percent.

Those numbers have declined.

In 1986, hospitals spent on average 6.5 percent of their budgets on charity care, the American Hospital Association says. By 1990, the number was 5.9 percent. In Pennsylvania, it fell from 3.5 percent to 2.9 percent, according to the Hospital Association of Pennsylvania.

Some spend even less. Methodist Hospital System in Houston made a combined profit of $76 million in 1991, and gave away $5 million in charity care—or 1 percent of its gross patient revenue. Its federal, state, and local tax exemptions were worth $36 million.

In Philadelphia and its four suburban counties in Pennsylvania, hospitals say they provided more than $169 million in charity care in 1991, including nearly $127 million in Philadelphia. They say this easily dwarfs the estimated $80 million in property taxes they are excused from paying. That's only one of their tax exemptions, however. And the $127 million includes bad debt—uncollected bills that the hospitals contend is charity.

In Philadelphia, which has more poor than any other county in the state, more than 96 percent of all care is paid for by patients, insurers, and government. Only 3.6 percent of hospitals' $3.5 billion in expenses went for charity.

"The fact is, there aren't many charity cases in the hospitals. [Patients] are paying for almost everything," said Allegheny

County solicitor Ira Weiss, who won settlements in lieu of taxes from several Pittsburgh-area hospitals.

"Most nonprofit institutions were founded by philanthropic people to take care of the poor. But I'm afraid the old Brahmins would be rolling over in their graves if they could see some of these hospitals today," Donnelly said.

"The days of the nonprofit hospital are over. They are vestigial institutions whose nonprofit form no longer has meaning," said Henry Hansmann, an attorney and economist at Yale University, who has written extensively about tax law and hospitals. "As a matter of tax policy, we may not want to do away with nonprofit hospitals, but that doesn't mean we still want to subsidize them."

These days, many medical miracles carry hefty price tags. Some high-tech procedures are so expensive that hospitals won't give them away as charity. Liver transplants, for example.

Linda Demko, a thirty-eight-year-old mother from the Pittsburgh area, learned in 1991 that her liver was so diseased she needed a transplant to survive. But Demko's husband, John, an unemployed steelworker, had no health insurance. And the couple didn't have anywhere near the $208,000 deposit required for a transplant by Presbyterian University Hospital, a nonprofit medical facility in Pittsburgh that specializes in liver transplants.

Linda Demko died on December 29, 1991, before her husband could arrange financial assistance. "She just went too fast," Demko said recently.

Bonnell Sirott, Presbyterian's associate director of finance, said, "We do not have a specific policy which provides for free transplants. However, we do work with patients to help them arrange payment." She said the hospital had tried to get the Demkos on Medicaid. "For reasons I don't know, the Demkos didn't start this process until very late," she said.

Even having Medicaid sometimes isn't enough. In February, Evelyn Zeller of Baltimore was turned down for a liver transplant by Presbyterian officials because Maryland Medicaid would pay only 70 percent of the hospital's charges.

"As you are aware, it is the policy of the University of Pittsburgh Medical Center that a patient be both medically and financially cleared to be eligible for transplantation," Barbara

Gannon, transplant credit manager, wrote Zeller on February 12. Presbyterian University Hospital is part of the University of Pittsburgh Medical Center.

"Medical Assistance of Maryland does not provide adequate payment for transplants performed at hospitals outside the State of Maryland," Gannon wrote. "The required deposit for a liver transplant is $208,000. Please be advised, however, that this amount does not represent an estimate of your total charges. You may find that your total charges significantly exceed the deposit amount."

"I don't have that kind of money and neither do hundreds of other people," said Keefer Zeller, Evelyn's husband, a pressman at the *Baltimore Sun*. "They do cases that make national headlines, but cases like my wife's, they turn their backs." Evelyn Zeller, fifty-four, is still looking for a hospital that will perform a transplant.

In November 1992, a jury awarded $3 million to the family of another Baltimore resident, Hugh E. Wilson, after concluding that Presbyterian had denied Wilson a timely liver transplant. The family contended that Wilson was passed over twice for an available liver, even though he had health insurance. Their suit said that hospital officials were concerned they would not get paid in full. The hospital and the family were negotiating with insurers when Wilson died on September 6, 1985.

Four days later, Dr. Thomas Starzl, a transplant specialist at Presbyterian, decried the hospital's handling of the Wilson case during a staff meeting. Notes of that session, which are part of the court record, reflect Starzl saying the case "showed an insensitivity . . . as well as bad moral judgment . . . in light of the money the program brings to the hospital."

Lawyers for Presbyterian have appealed the Wilson verdict and say that Wilson was not rejected because of financial concerns. A hearing is pending.

"When it comes to medical miracles like transplants, charity often fails to survive the wallet biopsy test," said University of Minnesota medical ethicist Arthur L. Caplan. "I call it the 'Green Screen.' What do hospitals do with high-tech procedures? They make sure only those with the ability to pay get them.

"Transplantation is where the world of nonprofit and altruism intersects with the world of high prices and high profits.

Organs that are donated by generous families are magically transformed into engines of profits," Caplan said.

Presbyterian spokeswoman Jane Duffield said the medical center "does provide a good amount of charity care, but not necessarily for transplants."

The hospital's IRS filing shows it gave away charity care valued at $2,620,136 in 1991. That was less than 1 percent of its $376 million operating expenses. The hospital's 1991 profit of nearly $32 million was more than twelve times what it spent on charity care.

Independence Blue Cross and Pennsylvania Blue Shield are exempt from paying state and local taxes as nonprofit organizations whose charitable purpose is to provide low-cost insurance.

Low-cost? Don't tell it to the Hills. Bill and Ruth Hill are paying more than a quarter of their annual income for health insurance from Blue Cross and Blue Shield. Since 1981, the couple's premiums for their 65 Special Medicare policy have risen nearly 250 percent—from $906 to $3,145 a year.

"We can't take much more of these staggering increases. We don't have a retirement or pension. All we live on is our Social Security and a little savings," said eighty-one-year-old Bill Hill, who lives in Northeast Philadelphia.

Thousands of other Blue Cross and Blue Shield subscribers have similar complaints. Many are abandoning the insurers. Since 1982, nearly 500,000 subscribers have quit because of rising premiums.

"It's no secret why these subscribers have left. It's expensive. We know that," said Blue Shield spokesman Doug Smith. Recently, the nonprofit insurers have taken several steps to hold down costs and make their insurance more affordable. Some critics say it's too little, too late. To them, Blue Cross and Blue Shield look and act like any for-profit insurer.

"What I want to know is what does Blue Cross and Blue Shield do to justify not paying taxes?" asked Ann Torregrossa, an attorney for the Pennsylvania Health Law Project, an advocacy group in Chester, Pa. "Thousands of individual subscribers can't afford them anymore. They've invested all kinds of money in for-profit businesses. Where's the charity?"

Congress asked the same question in 1986. It concluded that the health insurers—there were eighty plans nationwide at the time—no longer served a charitable purpose. Congress revoked their federal tax exemption and ordered them to start paying taxes in 1987.

Since then, more than half the states also have begun taxing the Blues. Like Congress, officials in these states have concluded that their Blue Cross and Blue Shield plans are no different from commercial insurers.

Pennsylvania is an exception. Its regulators continue to treat the four Blue Cross and one Blue Shield plans as nonprofit insurers.

The plans, whose revenues in 1991 were $7.8 billion, don't pay the state's 2 percent tax on insurance premiums. They don't pay state corporate income tax. They are exempted from sales tax. And in Philadelphia, Independence Blue Cross does not pay property taxes on its new $141 million office tower at Nineteenth and Market streets.

The value of these tax breaks for the five Pennsylvania plans totaled at least $160 million in 1991—and more than $600 million since 1987, the year the federal government began taxing the Blues. That $600 million would have been enough to provide doctor care and immunizations for all 320,000 children in Pennsylvania whose families had no health coverage—for four years.

Smith, the Blue Shield spokesman, said the Blues deserved their state and local tax breaks because unlike some commercial insurers, they accept subscribers regardless of medical condition. The plans also subsidize the premiums of some subscribers, especially older people who buy their 65 Special Medicare policies, such as the Hills.

"That's got to be worth something, doesn't it?" Smith asked. "Think what would happen if we didn't subsidize those policies. The costs would be much higher."

The cost of these subsidies is borne by other Blue Cross and Blue Shield subscribers, who pay higher charges. In effect, those subscribers pay a hidden tax so the insurers can hold down charges for individual subscribers.

The Blues' tax-exempt status in Pennsylvania has saved them millions. If Independence Blue Cross had to pay real estate taxes on its new Philadelphia office tower, its bill from the city and school district would be $3.4 million a year. The issue of whether the new building would be taxed went before the city's Board of Revision of Taxes in 1989. Lawyers for Blue Cross argued for exemption, saying the insurer had a "charitable purpose," and always had been exempt.

A representative from the city solicitor's office objected. "Blue Cross' primary purpose is to provide health care coverage to those who can afford to pay for it," T. Braden Kiser, then chief assistant city solicitor, wrote in a 1989 memo. "Blue Cross 'gives' only to the extent that it receives something in return— a regular subscription payment."

The board granted the property-tax exemption, despite the negative recommendation. The solicitor's office later filed suit in Common Pleas Court to challenge the exemption but did not pursue the case. A Blue Cross lawyer said recently that he thought the case was dead. David B. Glancey, chairman of the Board of Revision of Taxes, said he expected the case to be heard.

In 1991, Independence Blue Cross had revenues of $1.5 billion. Its cash reserves of $346 million would have ranked it, by itself, among the region's fifty largest firms.

Like other Blue Cross plans, Independence has invested heavily in for-profit subsidiaries. Between 1986 and 1991, it spent $29 million on acquisitions, which have lost an additional $18 million on operations. The biggest loser was Delaware Valley HMO. It has since been merged with another HMO and is now making a profit.

Collectively, Pennsylvania's Blue Cross and Blue Shield plans have invested more than $136 million in commercial spinoffs. They include health maintenance organizations, day-care centers, even a mail-order catalog.

As of 1991, the nonprofit insurers operated fifty-six separate subsidiaries, including forty-seven for-profit companies. By the end of that year, these ventures had lost $93 million, which subscribers' fees had to cover.

Like many big businesses, Pennsylvania's Blue Cross and Blue Shield plans have their own political action committees. In 1991, Blue PAC, financed by the Pennsylvania Blue Cross plans (and not Blue Shield), contributed $41,190 to politicians state-wide. In the first five months of 1992, Blue PAC gave out another $16,495.

State Senator Vincent J. Fumo, a Philadelphia Democrat, received $3,500 in contributions from Blue PAC. Fumo is a director of Independence Blue Cross.

Asked about the contributions, Independence Blue Cross said in a written statement: "Senator Fumo does an outstanding job in Harrisburg for the Philadelphia community and is a leading member of the state Senate. He deserves and merits the support of his associates at Blue Cross."

Asked why the state decided not to follow Congress's decision to tax the Blues, Pennsylvania insurance commissioner Cynthia M. Maleski declined to comment.

All this has left the Blues in Pennsylvania in a strange position. As Blue Shield spokesman Doug Smith put it: "We're a hybrid organization. That's a good word to describe us. We pay taxes at the federal level, but we're a nonprofit for state purposes."

CHAPTER 4

Why your kid can't afford college

It was cold in the Squam Lake boathouse in New Hampshire where they gathered that June morning in 1989. Even after the meeting was moved to a warmer room, a chill hung over the conversation. What would happen, one of them fretted, if the public found out about their meetings? Could they be accused of collusion? Indeed they could, another suggested: All it would take was some hot-shot government lawyer trying to make a name for himself. Things could get ugly fast.

Corporate raiders plotting a takeover? Wall Street insiders? Try college admissions officials.

They had met at the boathouse—officials from Harvard, MIT, Yale, Brown, Amherst, Dartmouth, Bryn Mawr, Smith, Mount Holyoke, and Wellesley—to compare notes on how much financial aid they would offer to selected students. Their purpose, as it had been for thirty years, was to avoid competing for the same students by offering better deals.

They called it an "overlap meeting." A federal judge called it conspiracy to fix prices, and ordered them to stop.

Antitrust lawsuits, hush-hush meetings, and soaring prices may seem more like big business than higher education. But these days, higher education *is* big business—more than $140 billion a year.

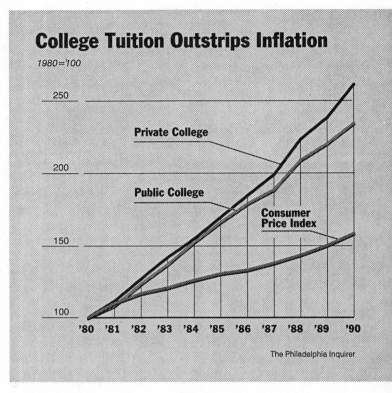

College Tuition Outstrips Inflation

1980=100

250

Private College

200

Public College

Consumer Price Index

150

100

'80 '81 '82 '83 '84 '85 '86 '87 '88 '89 '90

The Philadelphia Inquirer

It is also a profitable business. Some private colleges and universities bank $100 million a year after expenses. One has amassed investments of $5 billion. Some schools have become virtual research factories, under contract to private industry and government; they have spent heavily on buildings, high-tech labs, and high-priced scientific and technical talent. Others have invested widely in commercial businesses, including spin-offs from academic discoveries.

These costs have helped drive up the price of a private college education in the last decade by 151 percent. That's 2½ times the rate of inflation. Room, board, and tuition at a private university today can cost $25,000 a year. That would just about wipe out the after-tax income of the median American household.

Eighty years ago, Congress exempted colleges from paying taxes to foster and encourage education. Lawmakers also believed that a system of private schools would relieve the government of some of the burden.

Today, these tax breaks are worth an estimated $4 billion a year. But increasingly, taxpayers who help underwrite this subsidy—which is to say, all taxpayers, of however modest means—are seeing their own children priced out of the private college market or forced to absorb debts as high as $100,000.

As private universities have grown, they have changed in fundamental ways from the schools that Congress exempted from taxes early in the century. Consider these findings from *The Philadelphia Inquirer*'s eighteen-month study of the nation's tax-free economy:

- At some schools—including MIT, Cal Tech, and Penn State's main campus—more is spent on research than on instruction. As a result, some professors spend more time overseeing government and private contracts than they spend in the classroom.
- Colleges use taxpayer-subsidized facilities to help profit-making companies develop new drugs, cars, or computers, which then are sold to the public at big profits. The schools pay no taxes on this commercial income from their research and engineering work, and the companies get an R&D tax credit.
- Some schools have become venture capitalists, investing in risky, start-up firms. For example, Boston University has an investment of $75 million in a Massachusetts biotechnology firm, Seragen, which hasn't shown a profit yet and may never make money, according to Seragen.
- Schools have expanded the definition of education to engage in such commercial activities as catering, operating hotels, sponsoring trips abroad, running seminars and retreats, marketing computer software, and selling videos featuring star professors.
- Raising money has become a full-time business at many large schools. Princeton University boasts that its "fund-raising machine" brings in $1.7 million *a week*. Between 1981 and 1992, Princeton's endowment more than tripled and now totals $3 billion—enough to pay for tuition for its 4,550 undergraduates for the next thirty-five years.
- Sports programs at many large universities have become thinly disguised businesses, with multimillion-dollar tele-

vision contracts, highly paid coaches, corporate sponsor deals, and commercial endorsements.

- Universities are the largest private landowners in many cities. In Philadelphia, for example, tax-exempt educational institutions own nearly $1 billion in land and buildings that are not subject to real-estate taxes.
- Growing numbers of colleges and universities compete with taxpaying companies, supplying services that range from testing samples under a $1 million electron microscope to running simple laboratory blood tests. Owners of businesses say the schools have an unfair advantage because they don't pay taxes and use university facilities.

Just how prosperous some have become was pointed out by United States District Judge Louis C. Bechtle in Philadelphia, who heard the Ivy League price-fixing case. Bechtle ruled in 1992 that Massachusetts Institute of Technology violated the Sherman Antitrust Act by conspiring to control tuition prices in the case involving the financial-aid meeting at the boathouse in New Hampshire. Only MIT fought the case in court; the other colleges agreed to stop meeting after the Justice Department sued.

First, the judge had to decide whether a university, such as MIT, was subject to antitrust laws, like any business. Yes, he decided, because it engages in commercial activity.

"That MIT is a significant commercial entity is beyond peradventure," he wrote. "The magnitude of MIT's economic activity is certainly far greater than that of the vast majority of businesses." A $1.2 billion operating budget. Securities investments of more than $1.3 billion. Revenues from tuition of $158 million a year. Profits totaling $126 million.

MIT defended the sharing of financial-aid information by maintaining that the aid was charity, not commerce. Judge Bechtle didn't agree: "Although MIT characterizes its financial aid as 'charity,' in essence MIT provides a 'discount' off the price of college offered to financial-aid recipients. By agreeing upon aid, the Ivy Overlap Group schools were setting the price" these students would pay for an education. "The court can conceive of few aspects of higher education that are more commercial than the price charged to students," he wrote.

The price is soaring. At MIT, tuition alone stands at $18,000 a year in 1993. It rose nearly 10 percent a year between 1981 and 1991. The Ivy League schools—Penn, Harvard, Princeton, Dartmouth, Yale, Brown, Cornell, and Columbia—more than doubled their prices in the decade. Harvard, the wealthiest school with $5 billion in savings, charges $23,514 a year for tuition, room, and board.

The United States Department of Education has reported that in the 1980s the average cost of tuition at a private college increased 151 percent, from $3,498 a year to $8,772 a year. The average cost of tuition at a public college rose 129 percent, from $635 a year to $1,454.

During the same period, median family income of Americans increased 73 percent, or half as much as college costs. Inflation rose 59 percent in the 1980s, less than half the increase in college tuition. "It would be difficult to find a commodity or a service that rose faster than higher-education costs," said a 1992 report from the United States House Select Committee on Children, Youth and Families.

Almost nine out of ten Americans in 1991 believed increasing costs would put a college education out of reach for most people, a Gallup Poll found. "This perception—that college soon will be unattainable for most citizens—is an ominous sign that threatens the basic fabric of American education and society," the National Commission on Responsibilities for Financing Post-Secondary Education said early in 1993.

Tuition increases came as many of the wealthiest private schools were becoming wealthier. Endowment funds at the Ivy League schools nearly tripled in the 1980s, growing at an average annual rate of 11 percent, during a time of 4 percent inflation.

As they were raising prices in the 1980s, college officials were aware of the implications. MIT provost Paul Gray attended a meeting of Ivy League college presidents on December 7, 1983, according to his handwritten notes that are part of an exhibit in the government lawsuit against MIT.

At the meeting, presidents of the Ivy schools and MIT shared their anticipated percentage tuition increases with each other. Most were between 7 percent and 8 percent. "Some concerns expressed," Gray wrote in his notes. "(1) Are we pricing ourselves out of the market?" and "(2) Increase at 7–8% level will bring public criticism."

Those concerns did not stem the increases, though. The Ivy League schools boosted tuition an average 9 percent a year

Tuition at Large Private Colleges

Does not include room, other costs.
Adjusted for inflation.

College	1981	1991	Percent Change
Harvard University	$11,530	$17,152	49%
Princeton University	10,863	16,570	53
Yale University	10,713	16,300	52
Washington University	9,434	16,110	71
University of Pennsylvania	10,339	15,894	54
Mass. Inst. of Technology	9,290	15,600	68
Columbia University	10,039	15,520	55
Stanford University	10,698	15,102	41
Emory University	8,166	14,780	81
Rice University	5,536	8,018	45

SOURCE: Universities

Top 10 Private College Endowments

Adjusted for inflation.

Rank	College	1981	1991	Percent Change
1	Harvard University	$2,567,197,690	$4,669,683,000	82%
2	Princeton University	1,379,863,327	2,624,082,000	90
3	Yale University	1,187,592,079	2,566,680,000	116
4	Stanford University	897,496,568	2,043,000,000	128
5	Columbia University	884,625,743	1,525,904,000	72
6	Washington University	399,428,601	1,442,616,000	261
7	Mass. Inst. of Technology	749,530,026	1,442,526,000	92
8	Emory University	378,871,241	1,289,630,000	240
9	Rice University	564,675,611	1,140,044,000	102
10	University of Chicago	594,994,719	1,080,462,000	82

SOURCE: National Assoc. of College & University Business Officers   The Philadelphia Inquirer

between 1981 and 1991. In 1981, it cost $6,200 a year to attend MIT's classes, not including room and board; by 1991 that price had risen to $15,600. It was $18,000 in fall 1993.

At Princeton, tuition was $18,940 in the fall of 1993. With room and board, the cost rose to $24,650. A family paying for a child's Princeton education would be sending out a check for at least $2,054 a month for four years.

As Harvard president Neil L. Rudenstine said at the National Press Club in November 1992: "I seriously doubt that anything that costs more than one-third of a family's annual income, especially when you have to do it four years in a row, is what we would call 'affordable' in any usual sense of the word."

What accounts for these steep increases? Higher salaries and expanded campuses. And administrative bloat.

"Undetected, unprotested, and unchecked, the excessive growth of administrative expenditures has done a lot of damage to life and learning on our campuses," American University economist Barbara R. Bergmann, former president of the American Association of University Professors, wrote in 1992. "On each campus that suffers from this disease—and most apparently do—millions of dollars have been swallowed up."

The fastest-growing profit center at many large universities today is research. Consider Penn State University, a land-grant university that gets 17 percent of its $1.5 billion budget from the state. Penn State is second only to MIT in contracts performed for private industry—$35 million a year. MIT makes $43 million.

Total research contracts, both commercial and government-funded, in 1990 brought in $257 million, ranking Penn State ninth in the nation, after Texas A&M and before UCLA. At any given time, Penn State is working with four hundred companies on six hundred projects. Many of the relationships are confidential at the companies' insistence, the university says.

"Nearly one hundred research and development centers are housed within the university, many of which involve partnerships with industry," touts one of its promotional brochures. Researchers in one laboratory are at work for IBM Corporation, trying to make computer fans run more quietly. Their research is based on earlier Penn State work for the United States Navy on making submarines run silently. At another lab, researchers are working for a consortium of twenty companies to develop processes to coat ceramics with layers of crushed diamonds for grinding and other industrial applications. Yet another lab is working on the proteins given off by the roots of the Chinese medicinal cucumber. The Chinese have long used cucumber extract to induce abortions; researchers believe it also holds promise in fighting AIDS. Penn State is trying to interest drug companies in backing the project.

For large universities, such research jobs for industry can mean huge sums—Penn State collected nearly $147 million between 1987 and 1991. Tax benefits abound.

Universities pay no taxes on most of this research revenue. Companies subcontracting research to a university get a research-and-development income tax credit. And much of the equipment and technology was underwritten by state or federal dollars. The American taxpayer thus foots much of the bill, directly or indirectly.

The university also benefits from its own research discoveries through licensing fees and royalties on patents. This revenue also is free from taxes.

It is no wonder, then, that universities are spending more of their resources to qualify for contracts. At Penn State's main campus, research expenses were 30 percent of the campus's $179 million in expenditures in 1990, according to U.S. Department of Education data. That was more than the proportion devoted to instruction: 28 percent.

Between 1981 and 1991, research-and-development spending at universities rose from $6.8 billion to $17.6 billion, according to the National Science Foundation. Research spending grew an average of 10 percent a year. Industry-sponsored R&D grew even faster— 15 percent a year. The R&D work done for businesses more than quadrupled, from $294 million to $1.22 billion. Universities collected $7.8 billion between 1981 and 1991 from companies.

For companies, there are advantages beyond just the tax incentive. If a well-paid Ph.D.'s research is less than satisfactory, the university researcher simply doesn't get another contract. It's not that easy with a company's own research staff. And although companies pay for the research, they don't have to build the facilities, pay for the training, or increase their inhouse R&D. The universities absorb those costs.

Revenues from Research and Development for all Universities

Total Research and Development

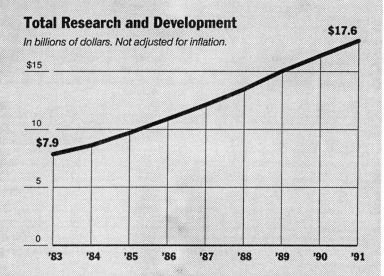

In billions of dollars. Not adjusted for inflation.

Industry Sponsored Research and Development

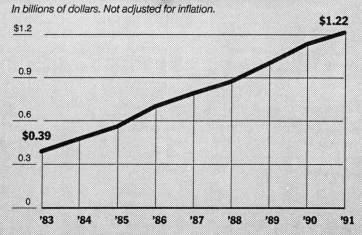

In billions of dollars. Not adjusted for inflation.

The Philadelphia Inquirer

As this commercial income was pouring into Penn State in the 1980s, tuition was increasing an average 9 percent a year. Undergraduate tuition for a state resident today is $4,548 a year—more than double the tuition in 1981.

About 14 percent of the research done at Penn State is for industry—twice the average for the twenty largest research universities. The balance is state and federal contracts. And the research business is expected to expand even more, as America's largest corporations downsize and cut into the budgets of their in-house R&D departments, said David A. Shirley, Penn State's senior vice-president for research. Shirley moved to State College in 1992, after serving as director of the government's giant Lawrence Berkeley Laboratory in California. He expects the industry share of Penn State's research could reach 30 percent in the next decade. The college has an all-out marketing program to attract businesses.

By the end of 1993, the first buildings will open at a 130-acre, $65 million research park near campus. Corporate tenants are being sought for the park, which will include a 150-room hotel and twelve-hundred-person conference center. Much of the project is to be financed by tax-exempt bonds issued on behalf of the university.

Will Penn State begin to pay taxes on the millions it collects for doing research? "I never thought of research as being taxable," Shirley said. "I don't think of it as a business activity. I think of it as part of the educational process."

In fact, there's a shortage of qualified graduate students to aid the research, he said. The university is considering increasing scholarship money to attract more.

Charles A. Garber says they've gone too far. The president of a commercial testing laboratory in West Chester, Pennsylvania, Garber has waged a continuing war against nonprofit, tax-exempt laboratories that are luring business away from taxpaying firms.

He and others contend that some universities are competing directly with taxpaying businesses for routine laboratory work, such as water testing or material analysis.

Garber formed Structure Probe in 1970 to analyze materials for clients under an expensive electron microscope. In November 1992, a newsletter from the Philadelphia Electron Microscope Society caught his eye. Near the employment-opportunities announcements was this "Services Available" notice: "A large university EM [electron microscope] facility is making their services available for contract use. Instrumentation includes a JEOL 330A SEM with Kevex microanalytical system and a TEM. For information, please contact . . ."

Although the ad didn't name the university, the electron microscope lab is at the University of Pennsylvania, and the notice was placed by two researchers, who included two telephone numbers at the university.

"Unfair? Of course!" Garber said in a letter to the newsletter's editor. "The university has its equipment purchased for it by the taxpayers of the United States, either directly or indirectly. It was put there for educational purposes only, and it certainly was not put there to be used as a commercial business, and in direct competition with for-profit tax-paying firms," he wrote. Copies were sent to Penn president Sheldon Hackney and to Garber's congressman and state representative.

The Penn staff members who were soliciting business have been told that it is university policy not to compete with for-profit businesses, said Phyllis Holtzman of Penn's news and public affairs office.

"A nonprofit has its tax-exempt status because it is to serve the public," said Earl H. Hess, chief executive officer at Lancaster Laboratories. "When that [tax exemption] is taken and twisted around to compete against the commercial marketplace, that's where we run into trouble."

Hess also has been battling nonprofits. His testing lab in Lancaster, Pa., was founded in 1961 and has five hundred employees. He said there were many instances over the years in which universities competed with his firm for both commercial and government contracts. "I wonder how that is fulfilling their mission," he asked. Entrepreneurs in private business are finding that universities with tax exemptions, state funding, and "what amounts to slave labor" in graduate students working in university labs are showing up as bidders competing for the same contracts, Hess said.

At Structure Probe, Garber maintained that Penn State also has crossed the line. "Penn State is moving in a direction that sort of obscures the line that separates what a business should be doing and what a university should be doing," Garber said.

"The taxpayers are subsidizing what Penn State is doing and a private company couldn't be profitable competing against that."

Garber, who opposed Penn State's activities in congressional testimony and in letters to the state legislature, said university research should be limited to basic and fundamental research with new discoveries as the goal. Garber complained to State Representative Elinor Z. Taylor of West Chester that Penn State's Low Level Radiation Monitoring Lab was offering a commercial service. He included a Penn State letter to a Princeton company soliciting business, with prices attached. The price list notes that "customers may request their samples be given higher priority to ensure a faster turnaround time."

"Please consider contacting our lab when you need radiological monitoring services," says the solicitation letter.

"This is just plain outright wrong and is something that absolutely should not be getting done at a taxpayer-supported institution like Penn State," Garber told Taylor. "As usual, it is the small businesspeople who are going to be hurt the most when Penn State deviates from its chartered purposes and operates a business/commercial activity."

Taylor passed Garber's complaint to Penn State. "I think he has a legitimate concern," she said.

The lab "has always been conscious of a potential adverse impact on commercial operations," Marcus H. Voth, director of Penn State's Radiation and Science Engineering Center, responded. Voth described the lab as a "self-supporting entity." He said "charges for analytical services have paid the staff salaries, purchased new laboratory equipment, and paid for supplies, materials, equipment maintenance, and other operating expenses. The laboratory has simultaneously been used for academic research. The marriage between a cost-recovery public service and academic research has benefited both programs."

Many private firms don't have the expertise or equipment to test radioactivity levels in water, Voth said in an interview. Full-time technicians perform the tests in the lab and students are not involved, Voth said. Like other programs under the research umbrella, revenues at the lab are tax-exempt.

When state officials proposed in 1992 eliminating that year's $15.3 million state allocation for the University of

Pennsylvania's veterinary school, Penn officials howled. Without that money, they warned, the school, founded in 1884 and the only veterinary school in Pennsylvania, would have to shut down. Each year, they said in a blitz of publicity, the school graduates about 110 veterinarians and treats fifty thousand animals. It is one of only twenty-seven such schools left in the nation, they said.

What was not said is that $15.3 million is a drop in the bucket for this educational giant—the third-largest private school in the nation when ranked by total revenues. Or that Penn could make up the lost state aid with just *four days* of its revenues. If Penn had to cover the vet school's lost state subsidy, it would take a 10 percent bite out of the school's yearly profits.

Penn is both Philadelphia's largest private employer—16,645 —and its largest nonprofit property owner. It is not unique, though, among tax-exempt universities.

The ten largest private universities and their revenues, including their hospitals, in fiscal year 1990, according to the United States Education Department, were: Stanford University, $1.4 billion; California Institute of Technology, $1.2 billion; University of Pennsylvania, $1.2 billion; Johns Hopkins University, $1.1 billion; New York University, $1.1 billion; MIT, $1.1 billion; Harvard University, $1 billion; University of Chicago, $927 million; Duke University, $911 million; and Columbia University, $841 million.

In 1991, Penn's total revenues of $1.3 billion from the university and its hospital were greater than the sales of the Strawbridge & Clothier or Pep Boys retailing chains. If Penn were a publicly traded company, it would be one of the twenty largest businesses in the Philadelphia region.

As for the vet school, Penn provides only $1.7 million of its own money each year for the school's $36 million annual budget. Part of that comes from fees that animal owners pay to have their pets and livestock treated at the school—about $9 million a year.

Students from Pennsylvania paid $16,326 a year in 1993 to attend; and the state has provided a subsidy of $15.3 million a year. In 1992, the vet school's unreimbursed care for animals— charity, in essence—totaled about $300,000, or less than 1 percent of the school's operating budget.

It is still uncertain whether the state will continue to fund the vet school. Penn admitted a new veterinary school class in the fall of 1992 and plans to keep the school open to graduate the class. But Penn would eventually close the vet school if state money is eliminated, said John W. Gould, Penn's acting executive vice-president. "It's not something we want to do, but we would be compelled to if we didn't get that support," he said.

Gould said Penn also would stop accepting new welfare patients at its dental clinic in West Philadelphia if the state carries out a threat to eliminate $1.5 million in annual funding. Penn's tax-exempt mission isn't to extend charity care to dental patients in West Philadelphia, Gould said: "We are tax-exempt because we educate people and we do research."

Nurtured in part by tax breaks, by the economic boom during much of the 1980s, and by contributions, many private colleges and universities have undergone phenomenal growth in the last decade. Their endowment funds—in essence, their savings accounts—have grown fat.

The growth is continuing into the 1990s. A survey of public and private schools by the National Association of College and University Business Officers found that among the 395 schools that responded, total endowment was $65 billion in 1991.

Endowment value of the ten largest private schools added together was $19.8 billion, triple the total a decade before. Harvard led the list with $4.7 billion.

Among the 286 private schools in the survey, the average endowment per student was $47,392. Princeton had the highest endowment value per student—$413,306, or nearly nine times the average. Between 1981 and 1991, Princeton's endowment increased each year an average 11 percent. Over that period, undergraduate tuition increased nearly 9 percent a year.

The University of Pennsylvania's endowment was $826 million in 1991. Although it wasn't as large as Harvard's, Penn's revenues were on a par. Penn's revenues of $1.34 billion compared with Harvard's $1.02 billion.

Of the $65 billion in total endowments in the survey, about 89 percent was invested in common stock and other securities, with the balance in venture capital, leveraged buyouts, oil and gas, and real estate.

Endowment funds of tax-exempt, nonprofit educational institutions are so large that they have spawned other tax-exempt, nonprofit corporations to manage all that money. Harvard has its Harvard Management Co., whose top employees are paid Wall Street–size salaries.

And one of the largest nonprofit corporations in the nation— the Common Fund in Fairfield, Connecticut—was established by a Ford Foundation grant in 1971 to pool the endowments and other investments of more than one thousand educational institutions. The goal is to maximize the return of each school.

In 1991, the Common Fund managed $11.6 billion in assets. Most larger colleges in the Philadelphia area participate in the Common Fund, including Temple University, Swarthmore College, Villanova University, LaSalle University, Haverford College, and St. Joseph's University.

In 1991, the fund collected $282 million in interest on savings, $319 million in dividends, and $270 million in gains from the sale of securities. Revenues totaled $909 million. Only $158,066 was declared as taxable.

Rebutting criticism of high tuitions, Harvard's Rudenstine and other educators point out that in the 1980s, scholarships funded with university money increased from $1.6 billion to $5.4 billion.

Financial aid *has* increased. But with tuition rising at 9 percent a year in some cases, students still are losing ground.

The *Inquirer* analyzed data collected by the United States Department of Education from sixteen hundred schools that listed how much scholarship money they gave in the 1989–90 school year from their own funds—not government or private scholarship and loan money funneled through the schools. On average, private colleges and universities gave away the equivalent of 7 percent of their revenues—not including university hospital revenues—as scholarships. MIT gave away 2 percent. Ivy League schools that were part of the information-sharing group with MIT ranged from 4 percent at Columbia to 8 percent at Brown. Penn gave 6 percent. California Institute of Technology—the largest private school when university hospital revenue is not counted—gave less than 1 percent in student aid. Johns Hopkins University gave 3 percent. Stanford University gave 4.

How Much Universities Spend on Scholarships

Percentage of the school's revenue in fiscal 1990.

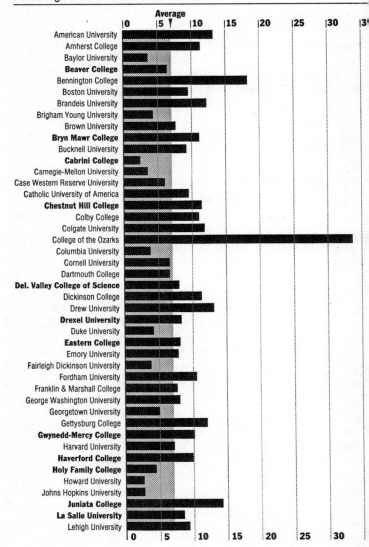

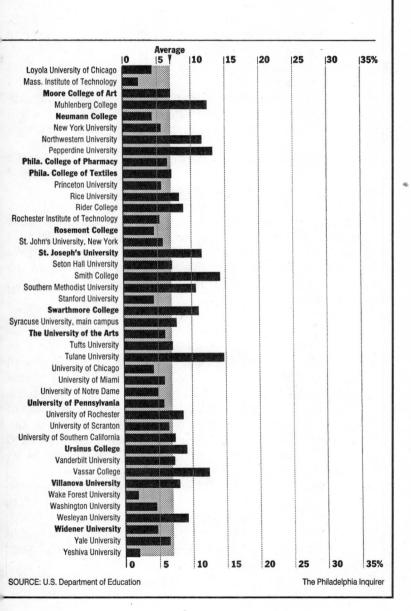

Average

	0	5	10	15	20	25	30	35%

Loyola University of Chicago
Mass. Institute of Technology
Moore College of Art
Muhlenberg College
Neumann College
New York University
Northwestern University
Pepperdine University
Phila. College of Pharmacy
Phila. College of Textiles
Princeton University
Rice University
Rider College
Rochester Institute of Technology
Rosemont College
St. John's University, New York
St. Joseph's University
Seton Hall University
Smith College
Southern Methodist University
Stanford University
Swarthmore College
Syracuse University, main campus
The University of the Arts
Tufts University
Tulane University
University of Chicago
University of Miami
University of Notre Dame
University of Pennsylvania
University of Rochester
University of Scranton
University of Southern California
Ursinus College
Vanderbilt University
Vassar College
Villanova University
Wake Forest University
Washington University
Wesleyan University
Widener University
Yale University
Yeshiva University

0	5	10	15	20	25	30	35%

SOURCE: U.S. Department of Education

The Philadelphia Inquirer

Although the big universities contributed relatively little, some schools—particularly smaller ones—were especially generous. One standout was the College of the Ozarks in Missouri, which devoted one-third of its yearly revenue to scholarship aid. In its annual rating of colleges, *U.S. News & World Report* has ranked it as one of the best liberal arts colleges in the Midwest. What makes this college different from most, though, is that students attend for free.

"Lack of funds should not keep students from attending college," the College of the Ozarks' catalog says. "The college will provide a way to meet the cost of education for every deserving student."

Nine out of ten students entering each class would have a difficult time financing a college education. The fifteen hundred students get a "free ride" by working fifteen hours a week on campus and forty hours a week in summer.

When they graduate, students may apply to their alma mater for scholarships to the graduate school of their choice. It can't be College of the Ozarks, which offers only undergraduate degrees. Two of the ten scholarships provide a free education through graduate school, which can include a professional school, such as law school.

"Confused about the economy?" the advertisement in the *Wall Street Journal* asked. For $295, busy executives could buy a half-hour video and watch the economist discuss everything from long-term interest rates to an analysis of federal economic policy. The tape was sophisticated—with animated fever charts showing the paths of indicators, a relaxed discussion of economic events over coffee à la *Wall Street Week*, and "Macrovision" protection to prevent copying.

What made this product different is its source. This video didn't come from one of the many economic consulting firms that make their living giving advice. This video was produced, marketed, and distributed by the tax-exempt Wharton School of the University of Pennsylvania—one of four produced each year starring Wharton finance professor Jeremy J. Siegel.

For Wharton and other schools, doing business outside the

classroom has grown as the college-age population has shrunk. As these tax-exempt schools have turned to broader definitions of "education," they've moved further into the marketplace, where they compete with taxpaying companies.

Wharton, for example, runs 120 seminars for forty-seven hundred executives a year. Penn State sponsors executive development programs at its State College campus; they last from two to four weeks and cost $1,900 per person.

Temple University is expanding its outside ventures. It offers courses in how to use computer software programs ("Profits and Losses. Creating a Budget Spreadsheet with LOTUS") for upward of $475 for a two-day seminar; how to use direct-mail marketing for $275; how to improve customer service for $225; and how to write a better business letter for $225.

Some schools have taken their seminar business on the road. California State University/Los Angeles has conducted seminars in fourteen states, lecturing on federal and state employment regulations. The cost: $595 per person.

In many cases, brochures advertising these services are mailed using a nonprofit organization mailing permit. Nonprofits in 1991 paid an average of 65 percent of what other organizations paid to send out second- and third-class mail—fourteen billion pieces a year.

Taxpayers make up the difference.

Nonprofit universities have invested millions of dollars in commercial businesses. Precisely how much is not known because the government doesn't require that it be disclosed. Some schools don't like to talk about that side of the education business. For example, the University of Pennsylvania owns interests in several businesses that aren't tax-exempt, including the Penn Tower Hotel. Other taxable ventures include University City Associates, a property rental company; Walnut West Associates, commercial real estate; Cabaret Company, a New York theatrical production firm; and Genesis, a Bermuda-based insurance company.

When *The Inquirer* asked for details on the businesses, the Penn Office of University Relations responded: "Your most recent request for additional information relates to the university's for-profit subsidiaries. As these records are not subject to inspection, we are respectfully declining this request."

Penn's commercial ventures were valued at $64 million and had income of nearly $18 million in 1991, according to its IRS filing. The university would not disclose how much, if any, federal income tax it paid on its taxable subsidiaries.

Large as it is, Penn's interest in for-profit companies pales compared with that of some schools. Boston University has invested heavily in commercial enterprises, including a biotechnology firm, Seragen.

Seragen got its start in 1979 as a joint venture between Boston University and several faculty members. The scientists wanted to develop and market monoclonal antibodies designed to fight specific diseases—then and now a promising technology. For financing, they turned to the university.

In 1987, Boston University invested $26 million in Seragen, gaining a controlling interest. Since then, the university has provided most of the working capital. When Seragen went public in 1992, the university canceled a $66.5 million loan to Seragen in return for additional common stock.

Following another stock offering in March 1993, Boston University controlled 60 percent of Seragen's stock—an investment worth about $75 million at then-current prices.

The prospectus for the initial stock offering warns of the risky nature of the business. "Products currently at the most advanced stages of development will not be available for commercial sale or use for several years, if at all," the company said in its Securities and Exchange Commission filing.

As of the end of 1992, Seragen had accumulated losses of $91 million. "There can be no assurance that the company will ever achieve a profitable level of operations," the filing said. Nevertheless, Boston University continues to bet a sizable chunk of its $337 million in investments on Seragen.

Seragen board members include many executives and trustees of the university. Chairman James M. Howell, former chief economist of the Bank of Boston, is on the university board of trustees. Seragen pays Howell $50,000 for fifty days of consulting a year, according to the SEC documents.

Another Seragen board member, John R. Murphy, is a BU medical professor and chief of biomolecular medicine at the university hospital. According to SEC documents, Murphy is paid $71,000 a year for consulting on "biotechnology matters."

And what has happened over the last decade at Boston University's other activity—providing an education? Tuition has tripled since 1980, rising to $16,590 in 1993.

A year ago, the United States House Select Committee on Children, Youth and Families set out to answer the question, "Why do college costs keep going up every single year?"

"The focus in higher education today is on research, not teaching," the committee concluded in a 1992 report. The study cited data from the nation's public universities, but noted that many of the same problems may be found at private schools.

Among the committee's findings:

- Labor costs have soared, in part because professors spend less time in the classroom. Faculty members used to teach fifteen credit hours a semester (about five courses). The load over time was reduced to twelve credits, then nine credits and "in many places it is six credits or lower" today. Colleges have had to hire additional teachers and teaching assistants to cover classes.
- Research has cut into teaching time. "A number of faculty avoid teaching altogether by buying out their teaching time with the proceeds from research grants or outside consulting."
- The school year now averages 30 weeks, and every seventh year many professors get a year off for sabbatical at full or partial pay. The average salary for a professor at a public university is about $63,000.
- Large undergraduate lecture classes are common. A marketing class at the University of Colorado had 618 students; a basic political science class at the University of Illinois/Urbana had 1,156 students.
- Administrative costs have increased sharply. In 1950, public colleges spent twenty-seven cents on administration for every dollar spent on instruction. In 1988, they spent forty-five cents for administration.

After the committee report was issued, the National Association of Independent Colleges and Universities dismissed it as "incredibly simplistic," said Timothy J. Morrison, the committee's chief investigator. Morrison said recently that he had received more than 150 letters and dozens of calls after the report was released—most supporting its findings.

"It's a profession that has not been criticized very much," Morrison said. But "it's an industry. I don't care how you slice it."

The University of Notre Dame collects about $1 million a game from NBC to broadcast its home football games. The National Collegiate Athletic Association hauls in more than $70 million for its member colleges from CBS Sports for televising the men's basketball championship for three weeks. The College Football Association negotiated a $300 million package for its members with ABC in 1990. All this commercial revenue is off the tax rolls. The colleges don't pay a penny in taxes on it.

To most Americans, it's no secret that big-time college sports are big business. But the IRS doesn't see it that way. As a result, you help subsidize these lucrative games in several ways.

College sports programs are conducted under a broad grant of tax-exemption. In essence, Congress and IRS ruled that college sports are not businesses or entertainment, but educational activities. As a result, hundreds of millions of dollars of income from television broadcasts, advertising, royalties, licensing fees, and ticket sales are swept off the tax books each year. And into the universities' till.

Take Notre Dame. In 1990, university officials signed an unprecedented agreement with NBC to broadcast its six home football games. The five-year deal was reported to be worth $35 million, or about $1.2 million a game.

"All revenue from athletic contracts is considered related [to the school's exempt purpose]. As an educational 501(c)(3) corporation, it's considered related. We don't pay taxes," an attorney for Notre Dame said.

Perennial football powers such as Penn State, Michigan, Miami, and Florida State routinely pick up millions of dollars from football broadcasts. Income from year-end bowl games, also tax-exempt, adds $50 million more to these schools.

Critics say it would be one thing if the profits from these events were used to lower tuition or pay teachers' salaries or were used for some other truly educational activity. But by and large, they are not. Usually, the money helps to underwrite other sports programs. Some of it goes to pay big salaries and bonuses for coaches.

The Knight Commission, a twenty-two-member panel that

spent a year examining the state of college sports, described it this way in a March 1991 report: "Within the last decade, big-time athletic programs have taken on all of the trappings of a major entertainment enterprise," with many high-profile football and basketball programs now "out of control."

"If anything, the problems of commercialization have only gotten worse due to the television money," says Richard L. Kaplan, University of Illinois law professor and tax specialist.

In the early 1980s, in the *Columbia Law Review,* Kaplan wrote that college sports at big universities are essentially a trade or a business. The commercial activities of other nonprofit organizations are subject to federal taxes; but not commercial sports activities of colleges.

"College sports have become a major money-making venture . . . with educational values largely peripheral to the activities," Kaplan wrote. "This has resulted in a double standard. Other nonprofits pay taxes on commercial ventures, while intercollegiate sports are exempt."

Chicago attorney Amy Forsythe says Congress is reluctant to remove the exemption because it would raise hackles of many voters. Forsythe questioned the broad exemption in a 1992 article in the journal *Tax Notes.*

"There probably isn't a congressman who doesn't have at least one of these schools in his district. I think they're afraid of what would happen if they went after them. College sports are one of the last sacred cows," Forsythe said in an interview.

Universities defend the businesslike approach of their sports programs as a fact of life. Profits from big-ticket sports are used to subsidize less profitable sports, such as field hockey, school officials say.

Sometimes schools use profits to subsidize nonsports activities. For example, at the University of Louisville, a separate, tax-exempt sports foundation has contributed $9 million to the university for general use in recent years, according to spokeswoman Denise Fitzpatrick.

Congress rewrote the tax code more than forty years ago to address the commercial issue. Legislators were concerned that nonprofits were taking advantage of their special status to operate profit-making firms and to avoid paying taxes.

In 1950, Congress rejected the nonprofits' contention that how they made money didn't matter, only how they spent it. A tax on the income from commercial ventures of tax-exempt organizations was enacted. It is called the Unrelated Business Income Tax. But a review by *The Philadelphia Inquirer* of 40 years of legislative history shows that Congress has never studied whether income from television contracts, licensing agreements, or royalties should be taxed. Absent guidance, the IRS has taken the position that income universities earn from athletic events is protected by the schools' broad grant of exemption as educational and charitable organizations.

One of the chief beneficiaries of the IRS ruling has been the NCAA, which describes its tax-exempt mission as governing and policing college sports. In 1990, its revenue was nearly $108 million, mostly from television broadcast rights, IRS returns show.

As the NCAA has grown, it has become more entrepreneurial. Today, it owns a separate marketing corporation, real-estate holding company, and foundation. The nonprofit, based in Overland Park, Kansas, receives millions each year in royalties and licensing fees from patents on its logos. One of its most popular markets is Japan. Most of the NCAA's money is spent on promoting sports—marketing, entertainment, collecting statistics, producing videos and highlight films, and lobbying legislators.

The Enforcement Department accounts for just 2 percent of its budget. The NCAA has fourteen investigators to cover one thousand schools—or one investigator for each seventy-one schools.

CHAPTER 5

IRS:
The cops that
can't keep up

In September 1987, a congressional committee investigating television evangelists asked Pat Robertson to testify about his Christian Broadcasting Network, which produces "The 700 Club."

Robertson, on the verge of entering the 1988 presidential race, told the panel he was too busy to appear. Instead, his son, Timothy, sent a letter that described the Virginia Beach non-profit this way: "The mission of CBN is to prepare the United States of America . . . and other selected nations of the world for the coming of Jesus Christ and the establishment of the Kingdom of God on Earth. CBN's ultimate goal is to achieve a time in history when the 'knowledge of the Lord will cover the Earth as the waters cover the sea.'"

CBN had another goal: building a profitable cable television network, The Family Channel.

Formed in 1977 by CBN, The Family Channel had grown steadily through the 1980s, attracting millions of dollars in advertising. By 1988, its revenues dwarfed those from the network's religious broadcasts. For every $1 generated by religious programs, The Family Channel's nonreligious programming brought in $4.50—more than $41 million.

Inside CBN, executives were concerned that the Internal

Revenue Service might crack down on the tax-exempt charity for becoming too commercial. They needn't have worried.

Drowning in its own sea of rules and regulations, understaffed and unprepared to audit large, diversified nonprofits, the much-feared federal service turned out to be no threat; it made no move to challenge Christian Broadcasting Network, let alone to revoke its tax exemption.

Nevertheless, CBN officials decided to act. In November 1989, Pat and Tim Robertson formed International Family Entertainment, a for-profit company, and put together a deal to buy The Family Channel from CBN for $250 million. They put up $150,000.

In 1992, the new company went public. Within hours, investors gobbled up 10 million shares at $15 a share. Overnight, the Robertsons' modest $150,000 investment became a personal fortune of $90 million.

It could have been a venture capitalist's dream come true—only in this case the cable channel was nurtured under the protective umbrella of a tax-exempt, nonprofit organization, underwritten for a decade by taxpayers.

Not that taxpayers had any idea they were helping the Robertsons build a television empire. Few understand that they subsidize the nation's $850 billion nonprofit economy through their taxes. In 1992, those tax breaks to nonprofit groups were worth more than $36 billion according to estimates by *The Philadelphia Inquirer.*

The Internal Revenue Service is charged with supervising this nonprofit economy. But an eighteen-month examination of tax-exempt organizations found that the IRS doesn't have the staff, money, or technical resources to adequately police the ever-growing number of exempt groups.

IRS's Exempt Organizations Technical Division, which is responsible for approving new exempt organizations and policing existing ones, in 1991 had 486 employees to watch over an estimated 1.1 million organizations—or one worker for 2,279 exempt groups. And that gap is widening. Between 1980 and 1992, the IRS approved 353,567 new nonprofits—an average of twenty-nine thousand a year.

While those numbers were growing, the staff of the Exempt Organizations section was declining: from 509 to 495 employees. In 1992, the number of nonprofit organizations had grown to an estimated 1.2 million. That raised the ratio to one IRS employee for every 2,424 organizations.

Nor has the IRS's budget for policing nonprofits kept up. In 1980, the agency spent $27.6 million to oversee exempt groups, or an average of $32.61 per organization. In 1992, IRS spent $35.7 million, an average of $29.75 per organization. Taking inflation into account, that meant IRS spending to supervise nonprofits declined by nearly 25 percent.

"There's always a budget limitation. That is part of life in any organization. Our challenge is to learn how to live with them and work with them," Howard M. Schoenfeld, a special assistant to the IRS commissioner, said in an interview.

Even when Congress asked if the agency needed more money to monitor exempt organizations, Reagan-era agency administrators in the 1980s turned it down. They testified before congressional committees that they had "adequate resources" to get the job done.

An array of data suggests otherwise. The number of audits of exempt groups declined sharply in the 1980s. In 1980, the last year of the Carter administration, the IRS examined 23,807 tax-exempt organizations. In 1988, the last year of the Reagan administration, it examined 11,907 nonprofits—a 50 percent drop. Under President George Bush, the number of audits inched back up to 14,891 by 1991.

Even so, with the rapid growth in new exempt groups, the IRS audited fewer nonprofits on a per-capita basis than a decade earlier. In 1980, it examined one of every thirty-six nonprofit tax returns. In 1991, it examined one of every seventy-four returns. Today, the agency examines about 1 percent of the roughly 450,000 nonprofits that file an annual tax form, known as a Form 990, with IRS.

Even that figure is misleading. There are another 750,000 or so nonprofits that do not have to file forms with IRS—exempt groups with annual incomes of $25,000 or less.

The IRS also counts each tax return that an agent examines as a separate audit—even if it involves the same organization. That practice inflates the overall count, because an agent who reviews three years of one nonprofit's tax return counts that as three audits. This makes it seem as if the IRS is monitoring more nonprofits than it actually is.

From Nonprofit to Big Profit

1977
- CBN Satellite Network, later renamed The Family Channel, formed by Pat Robertson's Christian Broadcasting Network.
- Religious programming.

1981
- Becomes advertiser-supported, entertainment-oriented cable network.
- Moves away from religious programming toward "family-value" programs.

1988
- CBN/Family Channel broadcasting revenue: $50.6 million. (Exempt revenues: $9.2 million) (Other revenues: $41.4 million)

- Concern about IRS scrutiny over growing commercialism.

1989
- Family Channel appraised in anticipation of sale.
- Broadcasting revenue: $62.8 million. (Exempt revenues: $7.7 million) (Other revenues: $55.1 million)
- Pat and Tim Robertson form private, for-profit company, International Family Entertainment Inc. (IFE), to buy The Family Channel from CBN.
- Pat invests $100,000; Tim, $50,000.
- Tele-Communications Inc. invests $22 million.

FOR PROFIT/PRIVATE • 1990 through 1991

1990
- Robertsons' IFE buys The Family Channel from CBN for $250 million in notes convertible to IFE shares.
- Nonprofit CBN pays no taxes on sale.
- IFE/Family Channel revenue: $93 million.
- IFE/Family Channel profits: $14 million.

1991
- IFE/Family Channel revenue: $114 million.
- IFE/Family Channel profits: $20 million.

- Salaries: Pat Robertson, chairman, $364,984. Tim Robertson, chief executive, $490,204.
- Pat Robertson remains chairman of CBN (nonprofit), collects no salary.

FOR PROFIT/PUBLIC • 1992 to present

1992
- Public stock offering (April) IFE/Family Channel 10 million shares at $15/share: $150 million.
- Robertsons retain control of IFE with 69 percent of voting stock.
- Their $150,000 investment becomes worth $90 million.
- 1992 salary, bonuses: Pat Robertson, chairman, $390,611. Tim Robertson, chief executive, $465,731.

- Pat Robertson remains chairman of CBN (nonprofit).

1993
- Family Channel plans to go international with versions in Great Britain and Korea.

The Philadelphia Inquirer

Monitoring the Nonprofit Economy

Expenditures
of the IRS's
Exempt
Organizations
Technical Division.

As the number of nonprofits grew—31 percent between 1980 and 199 —IRS's staffing didn't...

IRS staff
for nonprofit groups

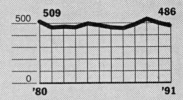

Ratio of nonprofits
to IRS staffers

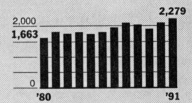

SOURCE: Internal Revenue Service

In 1991, the IRS reported it had audited the returns of nearly fifteen thousand exempt organizations. It turned out that after adjusting for double-counting, the IRS really had examined the returns of 6,011 exempt groups.

The audit is the principal tool the IRS has to ensure that groups aren't taking advantage of their tax-exempt privilege. The decline in audits indicates that the IRS has been unable to keep up with the growing commercialism of the nonprofit sector.

In the last decade, large nonprofits have invested billions of dollars in for-profit ventures, according to federal data and an examination by *The Philadelphia Inquirer* of six thousand tax returns. The IRS must rely on these tax-exempt organizations to report, on a special form called a 990-T, that they have taxable income—that is, income from businesses not related to their tax-exempt purpose. Interviews and records indicate that many large nonprofits fail to comply, or underestimate their tax liability.

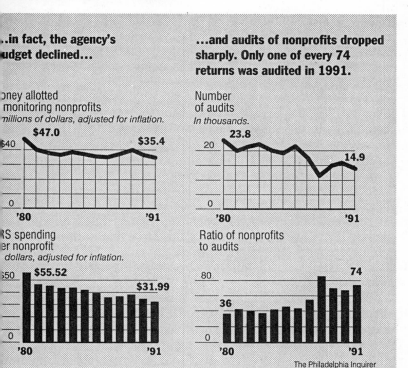

..in fact, the agency's udget declined...

...and audits of nonprofits dropped sharply. Only one of every 74 returns was audited in 1991.

ɔney allotted monitoring nonprofits
millions of dollars, adjusted for inflation.

$47.0

640

$35.4

0

'80   '91

Number of audits
In thousands.

23.8

20

14.9

0

'80   '91

ᴚS spending er nonprofit
dollars, adjusted for inflation.

$55.52

550

$31.99

0

'80   '91

Ratio of nonprofits to audits

80

74

36

0

'80   '91

The Philadelphia Inquirer

"A fairly healthy percentage of exempt organizations who ought to be filing 990-Ts don't," said Marcus S. Owens, director of the Exempt Organizations Technical Division. "A surprising number only filed after an audit has started. Of those who grudgingly admit they have some tax liability, we have found that 40 percent are going to underestimate their taxes."

Congress and others have begun to question the quality of the IRS's audits of large nonprofit organizations, such as hospitals and universities. In 1991, IRS and Treasury Department administrators acknowledged that the agency had been slow to develop sophisticated audit techniques. "Frankly, I think it took the IRS time to develop an audit program that was appropriate to the modern hospital," Michael J. Graetz, deputy assistant Treasury secretary for tax policy, testified at a congressional hearing.

In most cases, audits consisted of little more than a cursory review of a hospital's Form 990, another official said. "The depth of those audits has been pretty much confined to what is within the four corners of the information return that is filed by the hospital," assistant IRS commissioner John E. Burke testified in July 1991.

"We look at the hospital, we look at the operations of the hospital, and we have not gone into the transactions and the ventures and the subsidiaries that are controlled by the hospital so that we can offer a complete picture as a result of our examination as to what the hospital is doing," Burke said.

A lawyer for a large Philadelphia hospital characterized the audits more bluntly: "The field audits are totally worthless. The field agents don't know what they are doing. They only look at one entity. They don't track the money into the subsidiaries. There are a lot of awfully bright people in the IRS, but they seem to be stumbling." The lawyer added, "There's no way I or anyone else will tell you this on the record, for obvious reasons."

Owens does not dispute such characterizations. "When we did focus on large exempt organizations, we didn't have the resources and systems in place," he said. "We were missing things . . . and we were having many problems."

The IRS announced recently that it was stepping up the intensity of its audits of large hospitals and universities. Instead of a single agent going out to examine the books, the agency said it would send a team of attorneys, accountants, computer experts, and other tax specialists. "The idea is to put in place all of the concepts we use in our audits of the largest for-profit corporations," said Schoenfeld, special assistant to the IRS commissioner.

There is a catch. Because the new "comprehensive evaluations" are more time-consuming, the IRS expects to conduct only a dozen or so a year. And the number of overall examinations of nonprofits is expected to decline further.

In March 1993, Owens said twenty-three comprehensive hospital audits were underway. Some could take two to three years to complete. There are about thirty-two hundred nonprofit hospitals in America. Even if IRS could complete examinations of twenty-three in a single year, auditing all the nonprofit hospitals would take 139 years.

ongress, which periodically finds fault with the way IRS does its job, hasn't made the agency's job any easier. Over the years, Congress has greatly expanded the definition of charity and has moved to block enforcement action against selected nonprofits engaged in commercial activities.

Since the 1950s, nonprofits have been required to pay taxes on income-producing activities that are unrelated to their tax-exempt purpose. It's up to the IRS to determine what unrelated activities are and who must pay these taxes. But on half a dozen occasions, special legislation has been used to overrule the IRS when it did direct specific tax-exempt organizations to pay taxes.

Congress has ruled that income earned by nonprofits from buying and selling their mailing lists is not taxable. Congress has ruled that income nonprofits get from operating certain commercial television stations is not taxable. Congress has ruled that income nonprofits get from certain horse racing and parimutuel betting is not taxable. Congress has ruled that income nonprofits get from some trade shows is not taxable. Congress has ruled that income nonprofits get from bingo games is not taxable. Congress has ruled that income nonprofits get from operating an orange grove is not taxable. In each case, the decision was made on an ad hoc basis, frustrating efforts of the IRS to establish a clear policy on commercial activities of nonprofits.

Former IRS commissioner Lawrence Gibbs put it this way during 1987 testimony: "While I have no quarrel with the right of Congress to exempt certain income from tax, I would hope that in the future an attempt could be made to define unrelated business income in a way that would avoid the impression of a piecemeal repeal of the unrelated business income tax."

t was Congress, too, that complicated IRS enforcement by substantially expanding the definition of charity. Today, groups may qualify for exemption from taxes under any of twenty-five separate classifications. They range from civic leagues to farmers' cooperatives.

IRS examiners have little choice but to approve requests for exemption. This results in any number of interesting decisions. In recent rulings, IRS examiners agreed to exempt an association of Chinese software traders in California, a real estate investment firm owned by Harvard University, a group of Florida atheists, an association of Indian travel agents, and the Zoroastrian Society of Washington State.

And then there is the Council for National Policy, a conservative think tank. Following the election of Ronald Reagan in 1980, the council moved from Texas to Washington. It was granted tax-exempt status on November 9, 1981, as a charitable, educational organization. Contributions to the council became tax-deductible.

The council's primary activity consisted of holding several meetings a year for members and selected speakers at posh resorts around the country. The sessions were not open to the public. Nor were the remarks of the speakers generally published. Membership was by invitation only and often limited to high-powered politicians, executives, and members of the media. Membership fees ranged from $100 for associate members to $5,000 for members of the board of governors.

In 1990, the council's executive committee consisted of Reed Larson, president of the National Right to Work Committee; retired Lt. Col. Oliver L. North, the former White House aide; Howard Phillips, chairman of the Conservative Caucus; and Paul Weyrich, president of the Free Congress Foundation.

In 1990, the IRS questioned the exclusionary nature of the council. Two years later, the IRS revoked the group's tax-exempt status, saying it represented the private interests of its members and did not serve a public, charitable purpose.

The council appealed, and the case landed in United States Tax Court, which hears tax disputes. Following a flurry of initial filings, attorneys for both sides agreed to a ninety-day delay. Lawyers for the council had filed a new application for tax-exempt status, and the IRS agreed not to press ahead with the lawsuit until its hearings officers could rule on the new application.

"We decided that it was easier to make a revised application than to go through the expense of the court case," said Morton C. Blackwell, a former Reagan White House aide who took over as executive director of the council in 1991. Asked the group's purpose, Blackwell said: "We discuss public policy questions and bring in excellent speakers to share their information, and that information is used by our members and others in determinations about public policy questions.

"The IRS had said everything we were doing was legitimate. It was a question of whether we were serving a public purpose," Blackwell said.

The council's solution was to start publishing a semiannual journal of some speeches made at its closed sessions. The first issue of *Policy Counsel* appeared in the spring of 1992, with six essays by such conservatives as newspaper columnist Cal Thomas and economist Milton Friedman.

The IRS reconsidered the exemption. It determined that by publishing the journal twice a year, the council met its criteria for a public educational charity. On August 4, 1992, the IRS restored the exemption, retroactive to January 30.

Membership could still be limited to a select, powerful few. Its quarterly meetings could still be closed to the public. And the majority of its activities could still benefit only its members.

Speaking generally, Owens said that the IRS makes its rulings on a "case-by-case" basis. The more public an organization is, the more likely its activities may be viewed as educational, and qualify for exemption. However, sometimes a lawsuit or threat of a lawsuit may sway a decision, Owens said. "It's the hazard of litigation. You don't want to have a losing case on the record."

Congress's generosity in defining who qualifies as tax-exempt has resulted in IRS approval of nearly 354,000 groups in the last twelve years. Having created this huge shadow economy, Congress has paid scant attention to the consequences.

It has not conducted a major examination of the growth of nonprofit groups or their effect on the federal Treasury in a quarter-century. While Congress has held public hearings from time to time, the hearings' scope has been limited.

Even when Congress has addressed the subject, its actions sometimes have resulted in a windfall for nonprofits. In 1976, Congress changed the law that said foundations could remain tax-exempt only if they gave away, each year, 6 percent of their assets. The change? Congress lowered the requirement to 5 percent. As a result, between 1977 and 1991 an estimated forty thousand foundations were able to retain, rather than distribute in charity, more than $15 billion. In 1991 alone, the provision saved foundations about $1.5 billion.

Congress dabbled again in 1978. It took a hard look at the

fact that foundations were required to pay a 4 percent excise tax on their net investment income. Congress cut the tax to 2 percent. In 1985, Congress revisited the excise tax issue and decided that so long as foundations met certain other requirements, they should pay no more than 1 percent.

Congress has not always been so accommodating. On several occasions, IRS officials asked for authority to levy fines or penalties against nonprofits found in violation of the rules. Under existing law, IRS has only two choices in such a situation: Revoke the organization's exemption or do nothing.

Fines or other intermediate sanctions, Owens and other IRS officials said, would give the agency more leverage in getting nonprofits to comply with the rules. Congress has not heeded these requests.

Churches enjoy special tax-exempt status. They are not required to file an informational Form 990. And Congress has exempted churches and many of their related businesses from federal oversight.

The IRS cannot examine a church's financial records without undertaking complicated negotiations with the church. Even if a church agrees, the examination is restricted to a two-year period. "The standards for getting in to see the books and records of churches are a fairly tall order," Owens said.

This has resulted in any number of problems. First, the IRS does not know how many churches exist. It estimates that the number is between 300,000 and 400,000. Clearly, the IRS has no idea how much property or money is controlled by churches. Nor does it know how many churches operate travel tours, nursing homes, retirement villages, or other commercial businesses.

Virtually any individual or group may declare itself a church, collect money, and pay no taxes. "Unlike nonreligious entities, churches are entitled to exempt status without any requirement of filing a request for exemption. They are automatically exempt," James J. McGovern, associate chief counsel of the IRS, told a lawyers group in April 1992. "When other entities file applications for exemption, these applications and related materials are open to the public. . . . Because churches are excused from this general requirement, neither the IRS nor the general public knows who these organizations are or how many of them exist, let alone whether they are organized and operated under the rules of the tax code," McGovern said.

During the 1970s and 1980s, this led to a number of problems involving televangelists, whose broadcast activities fell outside federal scrutiny because they were considered part of a church—and therefore not subject to filing requirements.

Another problem: Policing compliance by religious groups with the rule against involvement in political activity. Churches are prohibited from engaging in political activities or election campaigns. But some have evaded that regulation by creating spinoff organizations.

After Pat Robertson failed to win the Republican nomination for president in 1988, he formed the Christian Coalition, a tax-exempt organization with more than 175,000 dues-paying members. The IRS lists the coalition as an organization engaged in social-welfare activities, a category called 501(c)(4). Such organizations are not supposed to engage in partisan politics.

According to news reports in 1992, the coalition took part in campaigns to defeat liberal Democrats, provided extensive support for pro-family conservative and Republican candidates, sponsored political strategy sessions, distributed voter guides, and worked to elect three hundred like-minded people as delegates to the Republican National Convention.

That fall, a complaint was filed with the Federal Election Commission, contending that the tax-exempt Christian Coalition was "avowedly and predominantly" into partisan politics. The complaint came from the Rev. Jesse Jackson's organization, the Rainbow Coalition. Christian Coalition officials fired back a letter charging Jackson's tax-exempt group with similar tactics favoring Democrats. So far in the battle of tax-free coalitions, the IRS has taken no public action against either group.

Even when the IRS moves against churches for political activities, it sometimes takes years. In 1986, evangelist Jimmy Swaggart used his pulpit and the official magazine of Jimmy Swaggart Ministries to endorse Pat Robertson's presidential candidacy.

Nearly six years later, in 1992, the IRS announced that it had reached an agreement with Swaggart's group to change its corporate structure and not endorse political candidates. In the interim, Swaggart was forced to resign his ministries after a highly publicized sex scandal.

The potential profitability of commercial enterprises owned by tax-exempt churches is documented in the growth of CBN. In the early days, the Christian Broadcasting Network was just that: a network of television and radio stations that carried Robertson's religious programming.

Robertson—minister, television evangelist, entrepreneur, millionaire, and presidential candidate—bought his first radio station in 1959. From that small entry into broadcasting, he used tax-deductible contributions from followers to build his program, "The 700 Club," and his broadcasting empire.

In 1977, Robertson formed the CBN Satellite Network—shows transmitted by satellite to the burgeoning, and at that time program-hungry, cable television systems. Four years later, in 1981, the network changed its name to the CBN Cable Network—The Family Entertainer. It became an advertiser-supported, entertainment-oriented cable network. The name was changed to the Family Channel in 1989.

Even as part of a nonprofit organization, the Family Channel was a fabulous money-maker, the crown jewel of CBN. During the last nine months that it was owned by CBN, the Family Channel's profits totaled $17.5 million.

Throughout those years, the Christian Broadcasting Network paid no federal taxes on its overall income. However, the network did declare the advertising revenues of the Family Channel as unrelated business income, subject to federal income tax. It could not be determined how much was paid in taxes.

In 1989—the last full year during which CBN owned the Family Channel—about $55 million of the organization's $130 million in revenues came from broadcasting. Advertising revenue and cable fees were growing. The amount earned from broadcasting was nearing the amount sent in by contributors, almost $60 million.

Robertson's followers, who donated more than $600 million between 1985 and 1990, were entitled to tax deductions for their contributions, and CBN was shielded from income taxes.

In a way, Family Channel had become too much of a success. By 1988, the channel was so commercially successful that CBN officials began to look into selling it, according to documents filed with the Securities and Exchange Commission.

The sale "arose out of CBN's concern that its status as a tax-exempt organization be preserved," says one of the documents filed by International Family Entertainment in connection with its stock offering in 1992. The document says that "by the late 1980s, CBN's revenues from The Family Channel had increased, relative to CBN's income from contributions to its ministry, to a point where CBN's tax advisers recommended that The Family Channel's operations should no longer be conducted within CBN."

Pat Robertson's own fears were described, after the sale, in an interview with a cable-television trade publication. "No one has told us we have crossed that line, but in our opinion we are coming dangerously close," Robertson was quoted as saying in *Broadcasting* magazine. "The big problem we face is that whole statute is totally subjective."

Subjective or not, the decision proved to be profitable for the Robertsons. In the deal, Pat Robertson put up $100,000, his son, Tim, put up $50,000, and Tele-Communications, the largest cable-television company in the nation, put up $22 million to form International Family Entertainment. The company, in turn, bought the Family Channel for $250 million.

In essence, CBN lent the buyer the $250 million to purchase the Family Channel, in the form of notes convertible into shares of stock in the Robertsons' International Family Entertainment. Not only did Robertson find a financier in his tax-exempt organization, he also found a low-cost financier. The notes' interest rate is 4 percent in the first year, 4.75 percent in the second year, and 6 percent in years after. And interest only—none of the $250 million in principal—had to be paid in the first five years of the loan, according to CBN's 1991 tax return.

Even after the public sale of International Family Entertainment stock in 1992, the Robertsons retained control over the company. Through shares he owns personally and shares he controls in trust for CBN, Pat Robertson controls 46 percent of the company. His son, Tim, controls 23 percent with stock he owns.

Today, the Robertsons' total investment in International Family Entertainment has grown from the initial $150,000 to more than $90 million. Of that, Pat owns—both directly and through the trust—shares worth about $59 million. Tim owns shares worth about $32 million.

Of Pat Robertson's shares, 77 percent is held in the Robertson Family Charitable Remainder Trust. Robertson retains voting and investment control, and thus beneficial ownership, of the shares. Any shares of the stock not sold before January 22, 2025, will be transferred to Christian Broadcasting Network, according to an IFE proxy statement.

Pat Robertson said that CBN's sale of the Family Channel was of "tremendous value" to CBN because the sale agreement guaranteed time for its religious programming on the commercial network. Robertson also said his and his son's compensation packages "are embarrassingly low by media industry standards." In 1992, Robertson said, he contributed 70 percent of his network salary to the nonprofit CBN.

Pat Robertson remains as chairman of the Christian Broadcasting Network. In 1991, CBN's tax return listed no compensation for him and said he worked forty hours a week at the nonprofit. He also has an employment contract with Family Channel's parent company, International Family Entertainment, that lasts through January 5, 1995, according to documents filed with the Securities and Exchange Commission.

As chairman of the public corporation, Pat Robertson in 1992 received $390,611 in salary and bonuses. Tim Robertson received $465,731. Tim, president and chief executive of IFE, no longer is listed on the tax return as an officer at nonprofit CBN.

The Family Channel also has continued to flourish. It reaches more than fifty-seven million American households—nine out of ten households with cable and six out of ten with television sets, the network says in its SEC filing.

And The Family Channel plans to go global in 1993. It plans to establish a version in the United Kingdom and is joining with Hyundai Electronics Industries Co. to establish a Family Channel in Korea.

All 50 states have laws regulating nonprofits, but very few actually police their activities. Nor do they have much information about their effect on the economy. States generally require nonprofits to file an annual report or tax return. State officials rarely audit nonprofit organizations or analyze their finances. In most states, officials would be hard pressed to say how many tax-exempt groups even operate within their borders.

Jurisdiction often is divided among several agencies. One agency may be responsible for registering charities. Another may determine which nonprofits are eligible for exemption from sales tax. Still another may decide which groups don't have to pay state income taxes. This helter-skelter approach can lead to policy conflicts.

Nonprofits that no longer are tax-exempt in the eyes of the IRS are still treated as exempt by many states. These states do not tax the commercial activities of nonprofits. The nonprofits also are exempt from paying sales taxes, yet officials acknowledge that their lists often are outdated and even include organizations that no longer exist.

Nonprofits also get discounted second- and third-class mail. Each year, about fourteen billion pieces of nonprofit mail—mostly bulk fund-raising solicitations and publications—are handled at rates less than individuals or businesses pay. That list, too, is secret. By act of Congress, the names and addresses of postal patrons aren't open to the public.

Efforts by the IRS to police the conduct of nonprofits can run into ferocious—and successful—opposition. Consider the Cotton Bowl.

In the summer of 1977, the IRS notified the Cotton Bowl Athletic Association that it planned to tax the revenues the association received for broadcasting the New Year's Day football game in Dallas. Reaction was fast and furious.

Although colleges and universities paid taxes on their purely commercial ventures, this was the first time the IRS had attempted to tax income from intercollegiate sports. Bowl officials and universities banded together in protest. With the help of lawyers and several members of Congress, they persuaded the IRS to drop the proposal.

Fourteen years later, the issue resurfaced in a different form. In December 1991, the IRS published Technical Advice Memorandum 9147007, in which it argued that the substantial fees companies paid to sponsor bowl games and other events could be construed as purchasing advertising—and thus taxable.

The memorandum did not name the bowl games or corporate sponsors in question. But it later became public that the memo was directed at the Mobil Cotton Bowl and the John Hancock Bowl.

Mobil Oil Corporation and the John Hancock Mutual Life Insurance Company had agreed to pay the bowls millions of dollars in fees. In return, the bowls agreed to use the corporate name and display the companies' logos prominently during the game and in promotions.

Again, the IRS decision to go after the bowls set off a wave of public protest. The bowl groups, universities, and corporate sponsors all argued that the publicity wasn't advertising; it was merely recognition of a donor's generosity. It was no different from public television recognizing Mobil Corporation, or any other donor, for helping underwrite a program, they said.

This time, the IRS didn't go after the income from television broadcast rights. Instead, it went after the advertising. In January 1992, the IRS issued proposed guidelines for its agents to use in examinations of such sponsorship arrangements. The guidelines required the agents to take a more aggressive view of the fees paid by sponsors and the benefits received in return.

The IRS was inundated with 339 written comments. Most were from organizations subject to the effort to tax sponsor payments, and almost all were negative. Sports groups were particularly incensed.

"The John Hancock Bowl has provided quality entertainment and an improved quality of life for El Pasoans for 58 years," the bowl organization's executive director, Cricket Musch, wrote. "The taxation of these corporate contributions would severely hamper our efforts to provide financial assistance to these . . . universities, which is our exempt purpose."

"The thrust of these proposed guidelines . . . misstates the law, perverts policy, and shows little, if any, understanding or guidance in corporate donation/sponsorship in the collegiate athletic field," attorney Philip R. Hochberg wrote on behalf of the Division 1-A Athletic Directors Association.

Meanwhile, friends of college football went to work within the halls of Congress. Senator John Breaux, Democrat from Louisiana, introduced a bill to protect corporate payments to "qualified athletic event activities."

Representative Ed Jenkins, a Georgia Democrat, introduced legislation to bar the IRS from taxing sponsorship payments to bowls and other big-time sporting events. "The guidelines threaten the vitality and viability of practically all tax-exempt entities and their local and national educational and charitable purposes," Jenkins said at a hearing in July 1992.

At least one of his colleagues remained unconvinced. "The Treasury is not saying that county fairs . . . should not be entitled to special tax treatment. What they are saying is that the college bowl system has changed dramatically in the last 10 or 15 years . . . way beyond what is appropriate for education," said Representative Mike Andrews, Democrat from Texas.

Initially, IRS officials held their ground, saying they were prepared to take the heat. "Maybe that's just the price we have to pay to get the higher level of voluntary compliance. Maybe we will have to draw a line a little inside where it could be drawn," Marcus Owens of the IRS said in a June 1992 speech to the Washington Bar Association.

And maybe not. A month later, IRS conducted an unusual three-day hearing on the proposal, during which it heard numerous complaints. Months passed without word on when the guidelines would become final.

On January 19, 1993, the IRS issued yet *another* set of proposed regulations. Under them, a corporate sponsor may enjoy nearly unfettered publicity without jeopardizing the tax exemption of bowl organizations. A corporate sponsor may:

- Demand that its name be used as part of the event.
- Put its logo around the stadium, on programs, on the playing field, on the players' uniforms.
- Require that the game be televised.
- Make sure that the cameras periodically show the corporation's logo/name.

Under the IRS's most recent proposal, these actions are not considered advertising.

And then there is the case of the IRS and United Cancer Council. The council was organized in 1963 by about eighty groups that had split off from the American Cancer Society. For twenty years, it relied on dues and contributions. But in 1984, the council entered a five-year agreement with a Washington fund-raising firm, Watson & Hughey, to solicit donations by direct mail.

In November 1990, the IRS revoked the tax-exemption of the Cancer Council, contending that it was operated for the private interest of Watson & Hughey, which purportedly received 90 percent of the money raised. Only about 10 percent of the United Cancer Council's money was used for charitable purposes, and its educational mailings were insignificant, the IRS maintained. Attorneys for the council say the contributions were greater.

In June 1990, the United Cancer Council filed a voluntary petition in bankruptcy, listing the IRS as a priority creditor. Less than a year later, it filed a petition in United States Tax Court in Washington challenging the IRS's decision to revoke its exemption.

Before the case went to trial, a letter was circulated by the Nonprofit Sector Legal Defense Fund, soliciting contributions for the lawyers representing the United Cancer Council and asking concerned charities to lobby the tax court. The letter accused the IRS of a "dangerous, blatant power grab" and said that if the service prevailed, it "would win the power to dictate how you run your exempt organization—and the power to put your organization out of business!"

Signed by the United Cancer Council's lead attorney, Leonard J. Henzke, Jr., the letter prompted a strong protest from the IRS, which asserted that it "wildly misrepresents" the agency's motives. It also drew a rebuke from the tax court judge, Herbert L. Chabot, who said the letter besmirched the court. The case is pending.

In a speech in September 1992, IRS associate chief counsel James J. McGovern attacked "confrontational" tactics now being used by some nonprofit groups and their lawyers. Citing the corporate sponsorship issue and United Cancer Council case, McGovern said these were examples of "how the game is being played in the nonprofit sector today."

It isn't entirely surprising that the IRS rarely revokes the exemptions of nonprofit organizations. Revocations are so rare, in fact, that the Internal Revenue Service said it couldn't provide a list of nonprofits that have lost their exemptions. "I have been told we don't keep them that way," IRS spokeswoman Johnelle Hunter said.

The IRS has revoked just one nonprofit hospital's exemption in the last ten years—a period when hospitals poured more than $1 billion into commercial activities and expanded greatly. IRS officials have said they are reluctant to revoke hospitals' exemptions because of the potential harm to communities. In essence, they say the penalty is so onerous they can't realistically use it.

The agency's choice is either to back off or to try to negotiate with the offending organization what is called a closing agreement—similar to a consent agreement. Increasingly, the agency is choosing the path of negotiation. But the negotiations can be painfully slow. Witness the IRS's extraordinary dealings with the Howard Hughes Medical Institute.

The facts of the case, culled from court documents, correspondence, and tax returns, are these: As far back as the mid-1950s, the IRS raised questions about the tax-exempt status of the Howard Hughes Medical Institute, eventually ruling in 1955 that it did not qualify as an exempt medical institute because it did not spend enough money on research. In fact, revenue agents concluded, the institute was actually an elaborate tax shelter for billionaire-industrialist Howard Hughes, who created the Bethesda, Maryland, nonprofit in 1953 and used it to shift taxable income into an exempt organization.

Incensed by the IRS's decision, Hughes hired the Washington law firm of Hogan & Hartson, which filed an appeal with the IRS. It was the first of a series of protracted negotiations with the agency.

In 1969, Congress passed a series of reforms intended to curb abuses involving tax-exempt foundations. One of them required foundations to spend an amount equal to 6 percent of their net charitable assets each year in order to retain their exempt status. The requirement was later reduced to 5 percent. Another reform imposed a 4 percent excise tax on foundation investment holdings, since reduced to 1 percent.

Attorneys for the Hughes Institute were still attempting to sort out its tax status when these reforms were passed. Their negotiations now took on added meaning.

If the institute were ruled to be a private foundation, it would be subject to the new spending rules and would have to dispense millions or lose its exemption. On the other hand, if the IRS could be persuaded to declare Hughes a charitable medical research institute, it would have to spend only an amount equal to 4 percent of its net charitable assets each year. For the Hughes Institute, that translated to a substantial savings.

Once again, Hughes' attorneys and lobbyists went to work, writing letters to the Treasury and IRS and working the back channels of the Nixon White House. Included in a July 1971 letter from Hughes lobbyist Robert Bennett to White House counsel John Dean was wording for a proposed grandfather clause to pending Treasury regulations that would have exempted the Hughes Institute from any spending requirements.

In August, Dean wrote Bennett a brief letter thanking him for "bringing this matter to my attention." He immediately asked Treasury officials to brief him on the case.

"The position of the Hughes Medical Institute is presently being given careful attention in this Department," Charles E. Walker of the Treasury responded on August 17, 1971. "We were not aware of their circumstances when the regulations were proposed, and I personally have met with their representatives. . . . No final decision has been made."

Treasury officials did not adopt the grandfather clause Hughes wanted. Nor did they declare the institute a foundation, which would have required it to increase spending dramatically. In essence, the institute was allowed to drift in nonprofit limbo, where it remained for the next sixteen years.

Finally, thirty-four years after the Howard Hughes Institute was created, it entered a closing agreement with the IRS on March 2, 1987. The exact terms are secret. However, details are contained in financial attachments filed as part of the institute's tax returns.

According to those and other documents, the institute had to pay the IRS $35 million for past years; distribute an amount equal to 3.5 percent of its assets for medical research each year; and make supplemental payments for research of at least $500 million by 1997.

On its face, the agreement seems like a good deal for the Treasury. But closer examination shows that the Hughes Institute actually got off fairly easily. For sixteen years, while the negotiations dragged on, it was not subject to the 5 percent-a-year spending requirements of a foundation. Although $500 million sounds like a huge penalty, it pales in comparison with the Hughes Institute's vast, untaxed wealth.

In 1990, the institute earned $309 million in dividends and interest on its $5.7 billion in investments—enough to pay off the $500 million in just two years. In 1992, the institute's holdings grew by 11 percent, and totaled $6.9 billion.

In brief press accounts of the settlement, institute president

Donald S. Fredrickson praised the IRS as tough negotiators. But his satisfaction was apparent. "It's been about twenty years and I think the service was tough, but I think they were pretty enlightened in the way it came out. We are not displeased with the result," he said.

CHAPTER 6

Charity pays: How much they make

As the head of one of Philadelphia's largest and most prosperous businesses, Edmond F. Notebaert was paid $433,200 a year in salary and benefits in 1991. He drives a Mercedes provided by his employer and lives in a $550,000 house, bought with a no-interest loan from his corporation.

Notebaert's profession? He runs Children's Hospital of Philadelphia, a nonprofit institution that is exempt from federal, state, and local taxes.

His is one of the higher-paying jobs in the Philadelphia area's $18-billion tax-exempt economy. High compensation is not unusual, though. Not among people like Iqbal Paroo, Gregory R. Anrig, or Richard D. Breslin.

Don't recognize those names? Many executives of nonprofit institutions aren't well known. Even less is known about their pay and perks.

As president of Philadelphia's Hahnemann University, Paroo is paid $493,898 a year in salary and benefits. Anrig, who heads the Educational Testing Service near Princeton, New Jersey, gets $383,968 plus use of a spacious house on the fringe of his organization's 351-acre campus. Breslin, president of Drexel University in Philadelphia, receives $300,189, including use of a university-owned house in suburban Bryn Mawr worth

$570,000 and a Lexus, maid service, and membership in two social clubs.

Then there's George H. Schmidt. He resigned as president of Main Line Health, the nonprofit parent of Bryn Mawr, Lankenau, and Paoli hospitals, all in suburban Philadelphia, in 1991. He had served 2½ years. Schmidt's severance package: $506,213.

Across America, executives of many nonprofit organizations are getting large sums in salary, bonuses, benefits, and deferred compensation, according to an examination by *The Philadelphia Inquirer* of six thousand tax returns of exempt organizations. Some get more than $1 million.

Officials say the compensation levels are necessary if nonprofits are to compete with for-profit businesses to get executives of the highest caliber. There is a central distinction, however: Salaries, mortgage loans, and other perks given to executives of nonprofit institutions are subsidized by taxpayers.

Americans reacted with surprise—in some cases anger—when it was disclosed in 1992 that William Aramony, president of United Way of America, had been paid $463,000 a year. He resigned in February 1992, and the United Way undertook a concerted effort to rebut the impression that charitable donations were financing a lavish lifestyle for managers.

An eighteen-month study of nonprofit organizations by *The Philadelphia Inquirer* indicates that Aramony's pay package was not unusual. The study—which also included an examination of court records, internal documents, and government audits—shows that the image of officials of nonprofit organizations as low-paid, self-sacrificing managers is woefully out of date:

- Nearly half of the twenty-five thousand executives and employees listed on the IRS returns were paid at least $100,000 a year.
- More than two hundred were paid $450,000 or more.
- Nine executives received salary, bonuses, and benefits exceeding $1 million, placing them in the top 1 percent of all taxpayers.
- Many large nonprofits commonly rewarded executives with cash bonuses and incentives based on the financial performance of their organizations, just as for-profit companies do. One large New York hospital paid its new president a $1 million "signing bonus."
- Retirement and severance pay for executives has soared.

HEALTH CARE

Pay Packages for Nonprofit Executives *As reported on IRS tax forms*

NONPROFIT ORGANIZATION / YEAR	NAME / TITLE	TOTAL COMPEN
Abbott Northwestern Hospital / 1991	Richard Bendel / Perinatologist	$
	Eric Knox / Perinatologist	
	Robert K. Spinner / President	
Abington Memorial Hospital / 1992	Thomas Dent / Chief of Surgery	
	David Eskin / Chief of Staff	
	Felix M. Pilla / President	
Albert Einstein Healthcare Foundation / 1991	Martin Goldsmith / President	
	John Murino / Senior Vice President	
	Robert Kimmel / Vice President - Marketing	
Albert Einstein Med. Center (Philadelphia) / 1991	Mary Ann Keenan / Chairperson	
	Robert Somers / Chairman	
Allentown Hospital-Leh. Val. Hosp. Ctr. / 1989	Samuel R. Houston / Secretary of Board	
Amer. Acad. of Orthop. Surgeons / 1991	Thomas C. Nelson / Executive Director	
Amer. Board of Internal Medicine / 1991	John A. Benson / President Emeritus	
Amer. College of Physicians / 1991	John R. Ball / Executive Vice President	
	Frank Davidoff / Assoc. Executive Vice President	
Amer. Health Care Association / 1990	Paul Willging / Executive Vice President	
Amer. Hospital Assn. / 1990	Carol McCarthy / President	
	David Woodrum / Executive Vice President	
Archway Programs / 1990	James I. Mason / Executive Director	
Assn. of Amer. Medical Colleges / 1989	Robert G. Petersdorf / President	
Blue Cross/Blue Shield Assn. / 1990	Bernard R. Tresnowski* / President	
	Douglas Peters / Senior Vice President	
Brandywyne Hospital / 1990	James J. Burnham / President	
Brigham Surgical Group Foundation / 1992	John J. Collins / Teaching Surgeon	
	Lawrence Cohn / Teaching Surgeon	
Brigham & Women's Hospital / 1991	H. Richard Nesson / Chief Executive	
Bryn Mawr Hospital / 1991	Darrell J. Bell / President	
	Carl I. Bergkvist* / Former President	
Bryn Mawr Rehab Hospital / 1990	Ken Hanover / President	
Cathedral Village / 1989	J. William Owens / President	
Cedars Medical Center / 1991	Paul Mass / President - Home Health	
Chester County Hospital / 1990	H.L. Perry Pepper / President	
Chestnut Hill Hospital / 1990	Cary F. Leptuck / President	
Children's Hospital of Philadelphia / 1991	Louis G. Troilo / Assistant Treasurer	
Children's Hospital of Pittsburgh / 1991	Edwin K. Zechman Jr. / President	
	William F. Donaldson / Medical Staff Director	
Children's Hospital/National Med. Center / 1991	Donald Brown / President	
Children's Seashore House / 1991	Richard Shepherd / President	
City of Hope National Med. Center / 1991	Sanford M. Shapiro / President	
Cleveland Clinic Foundation / 1990	Floyd D. Loop / Executive Vice President	
	Delos Cosgrove III / Surgeon	
Cleveland Clinic - Florida / 1989	Carl C. Gill / Chief Executive Officer	
Comm. Home Health Services (Phila.) / 1990	Adele Hebb / President	
Cooper Hospital/University Med. Center / 1992	Anthony Delrossi / Surgeon/Professor	
	Christopher Born / Surgeon/Professor	
	Kevin Halpern / President	
	Albert Tama / Executive Vice President	
Coriell Institute / 1990	Gerard J. McGarrity / President	
Crozer Chester Med. Center / 1992	Harvey Spector / Director of Pathology	
	Gerald Miller / President	

ALTH CARE

ckages for Nonprofit Executives *As reported on IRS tax forms*

IT ORGANIZATION / YEAR	NAME / TITLE	TOTAL COMPENSATION
ystone Health Sys. / 1991	John C. McMeekin / President	258,000
	Richard Thomas / Executive Vice President	216,340
er Cancer Center / 1990	George P. Canellos / Professor	193,413
Heart & Lung Center / 1990	Lynn McGrath / Surgeon	585,769
	Vladir Maranhao / Surgeon	411,346
Hospital Foundation / 1990	Julius Katz / Executive Director	115,000
Val. Hospital Council / 1991	John E. Flood / President	142,408
	Loreta M. McLaughlin / Executive Vice President	114,870
wn Hospital / 1990	Richard A. Reif / President	138,188
y Care Research Inst. / 1990	Joel Nobel / President	135,689
ue Cross/Blue Shield / 1990	Albert A. Cardone / Chief Executive Officer	540,000
	Donald L. Morchower / Executive Vice President	363,527
Hospital / 1990	Stanley W. Elwell / President	140,000
e Cancer Center / 1990	Robert Young / President	368,823
	F.J. McKay / Executive Vice President	236,665
n Health System / 1992	Ronald R. Aldrich / President	289,923
	Richard A. Long / President - FH Group East	247,346
Hospital / 1989	John B. Neff / President	222,222
ospital / 1990	James Delaplane / Director	154,986
	Malcom D. Strickler / Administrator	130,191
Clinic / 1990	William J. Krywicki / Associate - Orthopedics	663,899
	Albert D. Janerich / Associate - Rehab Medicine	502,646
	Arthur Sherwood / Medical Director	311,864
	Frank J. Trembulak / President of subsidiary	289,066
wn Medical Center / 1990	Hugh J. Maher / President	234,948
dical Center / 1990	David Leach / Physician	154,310
Health System / 1991	Harold Cramer / President	350,749
	Robert Mathews / Treasurer	289,385
	Robert Galloway / Senior Vice President	185,545
Hospital / 1991	Charles C. Wolfreth Jr. / Chairman of Surgery	200,000
w Hospital / 1990	Stuart H. Fine / Chief Executive Officer	115,000
alth Inc. / 1990	Frank Branchini / President	239,560
ck Medical Center / 1989	John Ferguson / President	182,063
nn University / 1991	M. Kerstein / Chairman of Surgery	385,642
	Harry Wollman / Senior Vice President	354,180
	Scott K. Phillips / Senior Vice President	333,054
ommunity Health Plan / 1990	John M. Ludden / Medical Director	324,028
	Thomas O. Pyle / President	288,478
urance Assn. of Amer. / 1990	Linda Jenckes / Vice President	245,927
t Inc. / 1990	David Buchmueller / President	257,308
emer Health System / 1990	Judith K. Call / President	141,381
ssociation of Penn. / 1991	Douglas R. Spurlock / Executive Vice President	329,657
	John A. Russell / President	222,600
or Special Surgery / 1991	Andrew Weiland / Medical Director	848,140
ughes Medical Institute / 1990	Graham O. Harrison / Chief Investment Officer	498,391
	Purnell W. Choppin / President	455,100
ealth System / 1991	Susan M. Hansen / President	126,145
ital (Philadelphia) / 1990	Paul Scholfield / Chief Executive Officer	130,399
m. Accred. Healthcare Org. / 1991	Dennis S. O'Leary / President	388,191
spitals / 1989	James A. Vohs / Chairman	511,511
rp. / 1991	Lloyd W. Lewis / Executive Director	150,206

HEALTH CARE

Pay Packages for Nonprofit Executives *As reported on IRS tax forms*

NONPROFIT ORGANIZATION / YEAR	NAME / TITLE	TOTAL COMPE
Lankenau Hospital / 1991	Elizabeth Avery / President	
Lower Bucks Hospital / 1990	Jose Samson / Physician	
Lutheran Gen. Health Care System / 1991	Stephen L. Ummel / President	
	George B. Caldwell / President Emeritus	
Magee Hospital / 1990	William E. Staas Jr. / President	
Main Line Health / 1991	Douglas D. Gregory / Vice President-Corp. Dev.	
Marshfield Clinic / 1991	Richard A. Leer / President	
Massachusetts General Hospital / 1991	J. Robert Buchanan / Chief Executive	
Mayo Found. for Med. Educ. & Research / 1989	W. Eugene Mayberry / Chairman-Development	
Mayo Foundation / 1991	G.K. Danielson / Surgeon	
	M.B. Farnell / Trustee	
Medical College of Penn. / 1991	Howard Zaren / Chief of Surgery	
	Henry H. Sherk / Chief Orthopedic Surgery	
	Paschal M. Spagna / Chief Cardiothoracic Surgery	
Mercy Catholic Medical Center / 1990	Plato A. Marinakos / Executive Vice President	
Mercy Health Plan / 1991	Felicia Neczypor / President	
Montefiore University Hospital / 1990	Philip Troen * / Physician-In-Chief	
	James Steinkirchner * / Chief Financial Officer	
	Irwin Goldberg * / President Emeritus	
Montgomery Hospital / 1990	John P. Cossa / Director of Medicine	
	Harry W. Gehman / Director	
Moss Rehabiliation Hospital / 1990	Randall Braddom / Vice President	
	Sy Schlossman / President	
Mt. Sinai Hospital (N.Y.) / 1990	John W. Rowe / President	
	Barry Freedman / Director	
Mt. Sinai Hospital (Philadelphia) / 1991	Francis Bonner / Physician	
National Bd. of Med. Examiners / 1990	Robert L. Volle / President	
	Daniel J. Klass / Senior Medical Evaluation Officer	
National Jewish Center for Immunology / 1990	Michael K. Schonbrun / President	
Nemours Foundation / 1990	John Noseworthy / Surgeon-In-Chief	
New England Medical Center / 1991	Jerome Grossman / Chief Executive	
North Penn Hospital / 1990	Robert H. McKay / President	
Northeastern Hospital / 1990	R. Moylan / Chief Executive Officer	
Northeastern Hospital Foundation / 1991	Francis X. Meehan / Chairman	
Osteopathic Hospital (Philadelphia) / 1990	J.H. Blackman / Chief Operating Officer	
	George D. Vermeire / Director of Clinic	
Our Lady of Lourdes Med. Center / 1989	John Capelli / Vice President, Medical Affairs	
	Alexander J. Hatala / Executive Vice President	
Palo Alto Medical Foundation / 1991	Robert W. Jamplis / President	
Paoli Memorial Hospital / 1991	Leland I. White / President	
Pennsylvania College of Podiatric Medicine / 1991	James E. Bates / President	
Pennsylvania Hospital / 1991	H. Robert Cathcart / President	
	James B. Hoyme / Medical Director	
	J. Douglas MacBride / Senior Vice President	
Pennsylvania Medical Society / 1990	Robert W. McDermott / Medical Director	
Philadelphia Heart Institute / 1990	Ami Iskandrian / Employee	
Philadelphia College of Osteopathic Med. / 1990	Daniel L. Wisely / Dean	
Philadelphia Health Services / 1990	Jose Galura / President	
Phoenixville Hospital / 1990	Richard E. Seagrave / President	
Pottstown Memorial Med. Center / 1990	Marvin J. Silverman / Director of Emergency Room	
	Larry A. Crowell / President	
Presbyterian Med. Center of Philadelphia / 1991	I. Donald Snook Jr. / President	

‹LTH CARE

‹kages for Nonprofit Executives *As reported on IRS tax forms*

IT ORGANIZATION / YEAR	NAME / TITLE	TOTAL COMPENSATION
	William T. Payne Jr. / Executive Vice President	110,700
gh Memorial Hospital / 1990	Marvin Mashner / President	119,000
art Hospital (Norristown) / 1990	Navin P. Shah / House Staff Physician	136,790
art Med. Center (Chester) / 1990	Glenn Hirsch / President	149,892
te / 1991	Renato Dulbecco / President	244,796
	Leslie Orgel / Professor	236,396
ara Medical Foundation Clinic / 1991	Arthur S. Greditzer / President	188,619
Chester Cty. Med. Center / 1990	Larry K. Spaid / President	139,930
Med. Center / 1990	Robert C. Fleming / Executive Vice President	120,634
-Riverside Med. Center / 1990	Joseph Trunfio / Senior Vice President	170,862
hildren's Research Hospital / 1990	Larry Kuhn / Chairman/Radiology	241,520
	Joseph V. Simone / Director	203,344
General Hospital / 1990	Edward R. Solvibile / President	127,659
spital / 1989	W.M. Tomlinson / President	176,155
rt Institute / 1990	James Cuthbertson / President	189,257
efferson University / 1991	Joseph S. Gonnella / Senior Vice President	363,796
	Paul C. Brucker / President	399,196
	Robert A. Peterson / Senior Vice President	292,360
	Thomas J. Lewis III / Senior Vice President	219,583
spitals Inc. / 1990	Myles G. Turtz / Chief Executive Officer	319,581
	Anthony Gigliotti / President	276,290
Cardiovascular Foundation / 1990	Harvey L. Waxman / Medical Consultant	247,053
Hospitals of Cleveland / 1990	James A. Block / President	273,599
Medical Service Assn. / 1991	John B. Downs / Anesthesiologist	282,563
of Maryland Med. System Corp. / 1991	Morton I. Rapoport / President	357,589
	Stephen C. Schimpff / Executive Vice President	258,113
ed. & Dent.-N.J. Foundation / 1990	James W. Aylward / President	128,276
. Health Services Foundation / 1991	John A. Jane / Neurosurgeon	460,409
	Neal Kassell / Neurosurgeon	460,409
Surgical Group Cincinnati / 1990	Tom D. Ivey / Surgeon	461,015
	Warren W. Bailey / Surgeon	474,206
r General Hospital / 1990	Frank Fumai / Executive Director	156,182
y Health System / 1990	Barry D. Brown / President	257,181
Inst. for Biomed. Res. / 1990	David Baltimore / President	314,394
lospital / 1990	D. McWilliams Kessler / Executive Director	128,081

JCATION

kages for Nonprofit Executives *As reported on IRS tax forms*

T ORGANIZATION / YEAR	NAME / TITLE	TOTAL COMPENSATION
llege / 1991	David G. Ruffer / President	$124,217
ege / 1989	Edward G. Jordan / President	132,308
ege Testing Pgm. (ACT) / 1991	Richard L. Ferguson / President	281,194
ollege / 1991	Peter R. Pouncey / President	172,700
chool / 1990	George W. Niemann / President	101,996
llege / 1991	Ellen Futter-Shutkin / President	261,748
ollege / 1991	Robert H. Edwards / President	173,321
ung University / 1991	LaVell Edwards / Football Coach	150,025
	Rex E. Lee / President	133,186
versity / 1989	Howard R. Swearer / Dir. Institute Intl. Studies	250,408

EDUCATION

Pay Packages for Nonprofit Executives *As reported on IRS tax forms*

NONPROFIT ORGANIZATION / YEAR	NAME / TITLE	TOTAL COMPEN
Bryn Mawr College / 1991	Mary Patterson McPherson / President	1
Bucknell University / 1990	Gary A. Sojka / President	1
Carnegie Mellon University / 1990	Richard M. Cyert / President	2
	Allan Meltzer / Professor	1
Colby College / 1990	William R. Cotter / President	1
College Entrance Examination Bd. / 1990	Donald M. Stewart / President	2
Columbia University / 1991	Eric Allen Rose / Surgeon/Professor	1,1
	Frederick Allan Rapoport / Surgeon/Professor	1,0
	Michael I. Sovern / President	4
Cornell University / 1991	Wayne Isom / Surgeon/Professor	1,7
	Karl H. Kreiger / Surgeon/Assoc. Professor	1,3
	Frank H.T. Rhodes / President	3
Curtis Institute of Music / 1990	Gary Graffman / Artistic Director	1
Dartmouth College / 1990	James O. Freedman Jr. / President	2
Dickinson College / 1991	A. Lee Fritschler / President	1
Dickinson School of Law / 1991	John A. Maher / Dean	1
Drexel University / 1991	Richard D. Breslin / President	3
	Dennis G. Brown / Provost	1
	Richard W. Schneider / Senior V.P. Administration	1
Duke University / 1990	Ralph Snyderman / Dean, Medical School	4
	H. Keith Brodie / President	3
	Phillip A. Griffiths / Provost	2
Duquesne University / 1991	John E. Murray Jr. / President	1
Educational Testing Service / 1991	David J. Brodsky / Executive Vice President	2
	Nancy S. Cole / Executive Vice President	2
Emory University / 1991	Charles R. Hatcher Jr. / V.P. for Health Affairs	3
	James T. Laney / President	2
Episcopal Academy / 1990	James L. Crawford Jr. / Headmaster	
Franklin & Marshall College / 1991	Richard Kneedler / President	1
Friends Central School / 1990	David M. Felsen / Headmaster	
Friends Select School / 1990	Richard L. Mandel / Headmaster	
Georgetown University / 1990	Robert B. Wallace / Chairman, Surgery	7
	John F. Griffith / Executive Vice President	2
	Rev. Leo J. O'Donovan / President	1
Gettysburg College / 1991	Gordon Haaland / President	1
Harvard Management Co. / 1991	Dave Mittelman / Vice President	7
	Jack Meyer / President	5
	Jon Jacobson / Vice President	4
	Vern Sedlacek / Treasurer	3
Harvard Real Estate Inc. / 1990	Kristin Demong / President	1
Harvard University / 1991	Daniel Tosteson / Dean, Medical School	2
	Derek C. Bok / President	2
	John McArthur / Dean, Business School	2
Haverford College / 1990	Tom Kessinger / President	16
Haverford School / 1990	W. Boulton Dixon / Headmaster	14
Howard University / 1991	Daniel O. Bernstine * / Gen. Couns.; Acting Dean, Law	43
	Carlton P. Alexis * / Executive Vice President	39
	Franklyn G. Jenifer / President	15
Johns Hopkins University / 1991	Michael E. Johns / Vice President	34
	William C. Richardson / President	32
Lafayette College / 1990	David W. Ellis / President	19

UCATION

ickages for Nonprofit Executives *As reported on IRS tax forms*

)FIT ORGANIZATION / YEAR	NAME / TITLE	TOTAL COMPENSATION
	Sarah R. Blanshei / Provost	109,080
Jniversity / 1990	F. Patrick Ellis / President	131,180
	Raymond P. Heath / Vice President Student Affairs	80,012
eville School / 1990	Josiah Bunting III / Headmaster	125,000
niversity / 1990	Peter W. Likins / President	231,350
	David Sanchez / Provost	156,600
	Roger Nagel / Institute Director	141,495
Jniversity / 1989	Niara Sudarkasa / President	111,385
st. of Technology (MIT) / 1991	Charles M. Vest / President	304,311
	Paul E. Gray / Chairman	289,007
	W.E. Morrow / Lab Director	275,400
ollege of Art / 1989	Edward McGuire / President	138,882
oke College / 1991	Elizabeth T. Kennan / President	209,752
Merit Scholarship Corp. / 1990	M. Elizabeth Jacka / President	149,158
n College / 1990	Nan B. Hechenberger / President	147,212
k University / 1991	John Brademas / President	436,610
	L. Jay Oliva / President-elect and Chancellor	379,843
	Saul Farber / Provost, Medical Center	364,385
stern University / 1991	Arnold R. Weber / President	284,709
me University / 1991	Rev. Edward A. Malloy / President	196,396
chool / 1990	Thomas DeGray / Headmaster	93,500
a. of Colleges & University / 1990	Francis Michelini / President	101,750
hia College of Pharmacy / 1990	Allen Misher / President	163,719
nior College / 1990	Raymond Lewin / President	105,000
University / 1990	Harold T. Shapiro / President	273,814
	T. Dennis Sullivan / Pres., Princeton U. Invest. Co.	211,421
	Hisashi Kobayashi / Dean, Engineering School	185,161
	Paul Benacerraf / Provost	181,633
College / 1991	Linda S. Wilson / President	143,386
lege / 1990	Frank N. Elliott / President	256,646
r Inst. of Technology / 1991	M. Richard Rose / President	197,568
er University / 1990	Joshua Lederberg / President	226,350
l University / 1990	P.J. Carlesimo / Basketball Coach	243,711
	Ronald Riccio / Dean, Law School	145,867
	Frederick Kelly / Dean, Business School	120,349
llege / 1991	Mary Maples Dunn / President	160,625
University / 1990	Norman Shumway / Surgeon/Professor	485,679
	Donald Kennedy / President	294,782
University Bookstore / 1990	Eldon Speed / Manager	112,500
h's University / 1990	Rev. Nicholas Rashford / President	115,500
ore College / 1991	Alfred Bloom / President	159,791
University / 1990	Richard F. MacPherson / Football Coach	273,431
	Melvin A. Eggers / Chancellor	241,167
	Geoffrey C. Fox / Professor	183,402
niversity / 1991	V.P. Addonizio / Surgeon	627,080
	L.S. Malmud / V.P., Health Science Center	443,752
	P.J. Liacouras / President	407,059
	R.J. Reinstein / Vice President	222,986
llege (Conn.) / 1991	Tom Gerety / President	165,550
ege / 1991	H. Chris Doku / Professor	325,457
	Jean Mayer / President	257,451
992	Charles Young / Chancellor	316,551

EDUCATION

Pay Packages for Nonprofit Executives *As reported on IRS tax forms*

NONPROFIT ORGANIZATION / YEAR	NAME / TITLE	TOTAL COMPEN
University of California System / 1992	David Gardner / President	
University of Chicago / 1991	Samuel Hellman / V.P., Medical Center	
	P. Warren Heeman / V.P., Development, Alumni Rel.	
	Hanna H. Gray / President	
University of Delaware / 1990	Russel C. Jones / Research Professor	
	E. Arthur Trabant / President	
University of Louisville Athletic Assn. / 1990	Denny Crum / Basketball Coach	
	Howard Schnellenberger / Football Coach	
University of Miami / 1990	F. J. Eismont / Surgeon/Professor	
	Edward T. Foote / President	
University of Pennsylvania / 1991	Alan J. Wein / Professor of Urology	
	William Norwood / Professor of Surgery	
	Luis Schut / Professor of Neurosurgery	
	William N. Kelley / Executive Director - Medical Center	
	Sheldon Hackney / President	
University of Pittsburgh / 1991	Michael Gottfried* / Football Coach	
	Wesley W. Posvar / President	
	Thomas P. Detre / Senior Vice President	
University of Rochester / 1991	Robert E. O'Mara / Radiologist/Professor	
	George D. O'Brien / President	
University of Southern California / 1991	Cornelius Pings / Provost	
University of the Arts / 1990	Peter Solmssen / President	
Ursinus College / 1990	Richard Richter / President	
Vanderbilt University / 1991	R. Bruce Shack / Plastic Surgeon/Professor	
	Joe B. Wyatt / Chancellor	
Vassar College / 1990	Frances D. Ferguson / President	
Villanova University / 1990	Steven P. Frankino / Dean, Law School	
	Rollie V. Massimino / Basketball Coach	
Washington University / 1990	Ronald G. Evens / Vice Chancellor	
	William A. Peck / Vice Chancellor	
Wellesley College / 1991	Nannerl O. Keohane / President	
Wesleyan University / 1991	William Chace / President	
Widener University / 1990	Robert J. Bruce / President	
	Anthony Santoro / Dean, Law School	
Williams College / 1991	Francis Oakley / President	
Yale University / 1990	Gary Kopf / Surgeon/Professor	
	Benno C. Schmidt Jr. / President	
Yeshiva University / 1991	I.R. Merkatz / Chairman of Ob-Gyn	
	David Zysman / Vice President for Development	

FOUNDATIONS

Pay Packages for Nonprofit Executives *As reported on IRS tax forms*

NONPROFIT ORGANIZATION / YEAR	NAME / TITLE	TOTAL COMPEN
Alfred P. Sloan Foundation / 1991	Ralph E. Gomory / President	$
Andrew W. Mellon Foundation / 1991	William G. Bowen / President	
	T. Dennis Sullivan / Financial Vice President	
Annenberg Foundation / 1991	Kathleen Jamieson / Dean, U. of Penn. Annenberg School	
	Peter Clark / Prof., U.S.C. Annenberg School	
	Walter H. Annenberg / President	
Arthur S. DeMoss Foundation / 1991	Nancy S. DeMoss / Chair	

UNDATIONS

ackages for Nonprofit Executives *As reported on IRS tax forms*

FIT ORGANIZATION / YEAR	NAME / TITLE	TOTAL COMPENSATION
Corp. of N.Y. / 1991	David A. Hamburg / President	499,497
	David Z. Robinson / Senior Counselor to President	243,477
wealth Fund / 1991	Margaret E. Mahoney / President	300,558
ndation / 1991	Franklin A. Thomas / President	545,255
	John W. English / Chief Investment Officer	506,235
	Richard Hopkins / Dir., Fixed Income Investments	414,298
Forum / 1992	Gerald M. Sass / Senior Vice President	215,042
	Everette E. Dennis / Vice President	200,107
Kaiser Family Foundation / 1991	Drew E. Altman / President	340,777
Endowment / 1989	J.H. Creekmore / President	152,266
therine MacArthur Foundation / 1990	Adele S. Simmons / President	349,144
etty Trust / 1991	Harold M. Williams / President	509,011
undation / 1991	James Spaniolo / Vice President	130,202
oundation / 1991	Alfred H. Taylor Jr. / Chairman	256,667
owment / 1991	Thomas H. Lake / Chairman	423,830
ritable Trusts / 1991	Thomas W. Langfitt[1] / President	620,862
	Rebecca W. Rimel / Executive Director	227,369
	Michael Rubinger / Associate Executive Director	157,003
King Mellon Foundation / 1991	Mason Walsh Jr. / Counsel	250,956
ood Johnson Foundation / 1991	Sidney F. Wentz / Chairman	277,075
	William C. Imhof / Chief Investment Officer	272,874
	Steven A. Schroeder / President	230,886
er Brothers Fund / 1990	Colin G. Campbell / President	237,170
er Foundation / 1991	Peter C. Goldmark Jr. / President	419,911
aife Foundation / 1990	Richard M. Larry / President	346,747
enn Foundation / 1991	Bernard C. Watson / President	185,000
ogg Foundation / 1992	Russell G. Mawby / Chairman	392,946
	Norman A. Brown / President	231,847
ck Foundation / 1991	Howard B. Keck / Chairman	624,500

LTURAL

ackages for Nonprofit Executives *As reported on IRS tax forms*

OFIT ORGANIZATION / YEAR	NAME / TITLE	TOTAL COMPENSATION
of Natural Sciences / 1991	Keith S. Thomson / President	$162,530
useum of Natural History / 1990	George D. Langdon Jr. / President	215,490
eater Arts for Youth / 1990	Laurie Wagman / President	178,000
ymphony Orchestra / 1990	Daniel R. Gustin / Asst. Managing Director	151,600
s Television Workshop / 1992	Joan Gans Cooney / Chair	546,686
	David V.B. Britt / President	351,763
Williamsburg Foundation / 1990	Charles R. Longsworth / President	269,282
Public Broadcasting / 1991	Donald E. Ledwig / President	116,532
al Brdcst. Corp. (WNET-TV) / 1990	Lester M. Crystal / Executive Producer	402,188
	William F. Baker / President	265,663
	George L. Miles Jr. / Executive Vice President	247,055
	Robert Lipsyte / Host	235,050
ommunications Inc. / 1991	Fred M. "Mr." Rogers / President	136,218
eum of Natural History / 1991	Willard L. Boyd / President	223,022
nstitute / 1991	Eric R. Aird / Executive Vice President	115,000
allet / 1990	Gerald Arpino / Artistic Director	130,967
Center for Performing Arts / 1990	Mstislav Rostropovich / Music Director	483,500

CULTURAL

Pay Packages for Nonprofit Executives *As reported on IRS tax forms*

NONPROFIT ORGANIZATION / YEAR	NAME / TITLE	TOTAL COMPEN
Longwood Gardens Inc. / 1990	Frederick E. Roberts / Director	
Metropolitan Museum of Art / 1991	Philippe De Montebello / Director	
	William H. Luers / President	
Museum of Fine Arts / 1990	Alan Shestack / Director	
National Gallery of Art / 1990	J. Carter Brown / Director	
	E. Roger Mandle / Deputy Director	
National Geographic Society / 1991	William Graves / Editor	
National Public Radio / 1992	Robert Edwards / Senior Host	
	Douglas J. Bennet / President	
New York City Ballet / 1991	Arnold Goldberg / Orchestra Manager	
New York City Opera / 1991	Christopher Keene / General Director	
Pennsylvania Horticultural Society / 1992	Jane G. Pepper / President	
Philadelphia Art Museum / 1992	Robert Montgomery Scott / President	
	Anne d'Harnoncourt / Director	
Philadelphia Orchestra / 1992	Joseph Kluger / President	
	Norman Carol / Concertmaster	
	Richard Woodhams / Principal Oboe	
Public Broadcasting Service / 1991	Bruce Christensen / President	
WGBH-TV Educational Foundation / 1991	Norman Abram / Talent, "The New Yankee Workshop"	
	Henry P. Becton / President	
WHYY-TV/WHYY-FM / 1991	Frederick Breitenfeld Jr. / President	
	Robert C. Prindible / Vice President, Finance	
	David Othmer / V.P. and TV/Radio Station Manager	
Winterthur Museum / 1991	Thomas A. Graves Jr. / Director	

CHARITABLE

Pay Packages for Nonprofit Executives *As reported on IRS tax forms*

NONPROFIT ORGANIZATION / YEAR	NAME / TITLE	TOTAL COMPEN
Amer. Cancer Society / 1991	William Cockrell / Executive Vice President	$
Amer. Heart Association / 1990	Dudley Hafner / Executive Vice President	
Amer. Lung Association / 1990	James A. Swomly / Managing Director	
Amer. National Red Cross / 1991	Elizabeth Dole / President	
Arthritis Foundation / 1990	Clifford M. Clarke / President	
Boy Scouts of America / 1990	Ben H. Love / Chief Scout Executive	
Christian Children's Fund / 1990	Paul F. McCleary / Executive Director	
C.A.R.E. / 1990	Philip Johnson / President	
Devereux Foundation / 1991	Ronald P. Burd / President	
	John O'Malley / Vice President - Clinical Affairs	
Disabled Amer. Veterans / 1988	Charles E. Joeckel / National Adjutant	
Elwyn Inc. / 1990	Marvin Kivitz / President	
Epilepsy Foundation of Amer. / 1990	William M. McLin / Executive Vice President	
Fed. of Jewish Agency Gr. Philadelphia / 1990	Robert Forman / Executive Vice President	
Federation of the Handicapped / 1990	Milton Cohen / Executive Director	
Girl Scouts of America / 1989	Frances Hesselbein / Executive Director	
Humane Society of the U.S. / 1990	John A. Hoyt / President	
Inglis House / 1989	David Romanoff / Medical Director	
Juvenile Diabetes Foundation / 1989	Gloria Pennington / Executive Director	
Lighthouse Inc. / 1991	Barbara Silverstone / Executive Director	
March of Dimes Birth Defects Foundation / 1990	Charles L. Massey / President Emeritus	
	Jennifer Howse / President	

CHARITABLE

Pay Packages for Nonprofit Executives *As reported on IRS tax forms*

NONPROFIT ORGANIZATION / YEAR	NAME / TITLE	TOTAL COMPENSATION
Mothers Against Drunk Driving / 1990	Robert J. King / Executive Director	123,187
Muscular Dystrophy Association / 1991	Robert Ross / Executive Director	291,593
National 4-H Council / 1991	Richard J. Sauer / President	130,810
National Abortion Rights Action League / 1991	Kate Michelman/Executive Director	99,711
National Audubon Society / 1991	Peter A.A. Berle / President	145,384
National Easter Seal Society / 1990	John Garrison / President	143,238
National Right to Life Committee / 1991	J.C. Wilke / President	110,525
National Wildlife Federation / 1990	J.D. Hair / President	289,341
Natural Lands Trust / 1990	Michael G. Clarke / President	89,790
Nature Conservancy / 1991	John C. Sawhill / President	196,576
North Shore Animal League / 1990	David J. Ganz / Executive Director	180,833
Philadelphia Corp. for Aging / 1990	Rodney D. Williams / Executive	89,097
Save the Children Federation / 1990	James Bausch / President	229,304
Sierra Club / 1990	Michael L. Fischer / Executive Director	107,500
Sierra Club Legal Defense Fund / 1990	Fredric P. Sutherland / President	157,219
Southern Poverty Law Center / 1990	Richard Cohen / Legal Director	122,036
	Morris Dees Jr. / Chief Trial Counsel	104,451
Ellis Island Foundation / 1990	Stephen A. Birganti / President	157,658
UNICEF / 1991	Lawrence E. Bruce Jr. / President	175,500
United Negro College Fund / 1990	Christopher F. Edley / President	117,527
United Service Organizations (USO) / 1990	Charles T. Hagel / President	179,280
United Way of America / 1990	William Aramony / President	413,463
	Frederick Cerny* / Regional Director	219,836
United Way of S.E. Pennsylvania / 1992	Ted L. Moore / President	205,348
	A.J. Sassone / Vice President	143,392
	Francis A. Marzolf / Managing Director	111,653
Up With People / 1990	J. Blanton Belk / President	141,750
YMCA - Philadelphia / 1990	D. Allan Shaffer / President	154,145

TRADE GROUPS, RESEARCH

Pay Packages for Nonprofit Executives *As reported on IRS tax forms*

NONPROFIT ORGANIZATION / YEAR	NAME / TITLE	TOTAL COMPENSATION
AFL-CIO / 1991	Lane Kirkland / President	$174,275
Amer. Arbitration Association / 1990	Robert Coulson / President	186,007
Amer. Assn. of Retired Persons / 1990	Horace B. Deets / Executive Director	258,252
Amer. Council of Life Insurance / 1991	W. Kingsley / Executive Vice President	301,949
Amer. Enterprise Institute / 1989	Christopher C. DeMuth / President	251,161
Amer. Family Association / 1991	Don Wildmon / President	121,635
Amer. Frozen Food Institute / 1991	Steven C. Anderson / President	137,376
Amer. Iron and Steel Inst. / 1991	M. Deaner / President	236,000
Amer. Law Institute / 1990	Paul Wolkin / Executive Vice President	205,625
Amer. Management Association / 1991	Thomas R. Horton / Chief Executive Officer	338,074
Amer. Soc. for Technion / 1989	Melvyn Bloom / Executive Vice President	230,489
Amer. Soc. for Testing & Materials / 1990	Joseph G. O'Grady / President	121,401
Amer. Soc. of Assn. Executives / 1991	R.W. Taylor / President	325,098
Analytic Services Inc. / 1991	John A. Englund / President	213,564
Assn. of Amer. Public TV Stations / 1991	David J. Brugger / President	161,314
Athletic Congress/USA / 1990	Ollan Cassell / Executive Director	119,603
Atlanta Comm. for Olympic Games / 1992	William Payne / President	530,000
Biological Abstracts / 1990	H.E. Kennedy / President	152,252

TRADE GROUPS, RESEARCH

Pay Packages for Nonprofit Executives *As reported on IRS tax forms*

NONPROFIT ORGANIZATION / YEAR	NAME / TITLE	TOTAL COMPENSATION
Carnegie Institute / 1990	Robert C. Wilburn / President	113,038
Charles Stark Draper Laboratory / 1991	Michele S. Sapuppo / Director	290,320
	Ralph H. Jacobson / President	231,642
College Football Association / 1991	Charles M. Neinas / Executive Director	189,059
College Retire. & Equities Fund / 1990	James S. Martin / Executive Vice President	1,098,529
	C. Oscar Morong Jr. / Senior Vice President	825,691
	Virgil Cumming / Senior Vice President	640,600
Common Fund for Nonprofit Org. / 1991	George F. Keane / President	509,076
	David K. Storrs / Senior Vice President	270,612
Conference Board / 1990	Preston Townley / President	266,553
Consortium for Sci. Computing / 1990	Doyle D. Knight / President	127,900
Consumers Union / 1990	Rhoda H. Karpatkin / Executive Director	177,979
Cottonbowl Athletic Assn. / 1990	Jim Brock / Executive Vice President	118,528
Cousteau Society / 1990	Jean-Michael Cousteau / Executive Vice President	166,427
	Paula DiPerna / Writer/Producer	106,024
Edison Electric Institute / 1990	T. Kuhn / Executive Vice President	209,324
Eisenhower Exchange Fellowships / 1990	Theodore W. Friend / President	95,000
Financial Accounting Foundation (FASB) / 1990	D.R. Beresford / Chairman	414,218
	R.C. Lauver / Member, Fin. Acctg. Standards Bd.	378,546
Free Congress Res. & Educ. Foundation / 1991	Paul M. Weyrich / President	179,209
Greater Philadelphia Chamber Commerce / 1990	Charles P. Pizzi / President	129,990
Greater Philadelphia First Corp. / 1990	John Claypool / Executive Director	99,570
Guideposts Associates / 1990	Wendell Forbes / Deputy Publisher	158,479
Heritage Foundation / 1990	Edwin J. Feulner Jr. / President	342,644
	Edwin Meese / Reagan Fellow in Public Policy	221,780
Home Builders Institute / 1990	Philip Polirchak / President	173,016
IIT Research Institute / 1991	John B. Scott / President	228,038
Independent Sector / 1991	Brian O'Connell / President	221,757
Major League Baseball Players Assn. / 1990	Donald M. Fehr / Executive Director	506,916
Mitre Corp. / 1991	Harold W. Sorenson / Group Vice President	206,770
Monell Chemical Senses / 1990	Morley R. Kare / President	109,056
Motion Picture Assn. of Amer. / 1991	Myron Karlin / Executive Vice President	575,456
Mutual of Amer. Life Insurance Co. / 1991	Joan Casson / Executive Vice President	264,652
	Howard Lichtenstein / Executive Vice President	254,577
National Academy of Sciences / 1991	Frank Press / President	328,295
	Robert M. White / President, National Acad. Engineering	294,474
National Assn. Manufacturers / 1990	Jerry Jasinowski / President	215,687
National Assn. of Realtors / 1990	William D. North / Executive Vice President	321,416
National Bureau of Econ. Res. / 1990	Martin Feldstein / President	222,600
National Cable Television Assn. / 1990	James P. Mooney / President	448,433
National Council on the Aging / 1990	Daniel Thursz / President	116,270
National Education Association / 1990	Keith Geiger / President	165,697
National Football League / 1992	Jay Moyer / Executive Vice President	380,000
National Football League Players Assn. / 1991	Gene Upshaw / Executive Director	297,055
National Hockey League / 1990	John A. Ziegler Jr. / President	500,000
	Gilbert Stein / Vice President	215,000
National Opinion Research Center / 1990	Richard Kulka / Assistant Technical Director	109,648
National Resources Defense Council / 1991	John H. Adams / Executive Director	138,296
National Trust for Historic Pres. / 1990	J. Jackson Walter / President	207,019
National Urban League / 1990	John Jacob / President	109,999
National Abortion Rights Action League / 1991	Kate Michelman / Executive Director	99,711

TRADE GROUPS, RESEARCH

Pay Packages for Nonprofit Executives *As reported on IRS tax forms*

NONPROFIT ORGANIZATION / YEAR	NAME / TITLE	TOTAL COMPENSATION
National Assn. Exch. of Indus. Resrces. / 1990	Norbert C. Smith / Chairman	212,693
Natural Resources Defense Council / 1991	John H. Adams / Executive Director	138,296
Naval Academy Athletic Assn. / 1991	George R. Chaump / Football Coach	142,871
Nellie Mae Inc. / 1990	Lawrence W. O'Toole / President	281,704
New York Shipping Assn. / 1991	James A. Capo / President	182,722
Newspaper Advertising Bureau / 1991	Leonard P. Forman / President	334,021
NSF International / 1991	Nina I. McClelland / President	164,667
Outward Bound / 1990	John Reynolds / President	132,405
Penns Landing Corp. / 1991	Dominic Sabatini / Managing Director	117,292
Pennsylvania Compensation Rating Bureau / 1990	Timothy L. Wisecarver / President	133,046
Pennsylvania Economy League / 1991	Dianne E. Reed / Executive Director - Eastern Division	86,750
Philadelphia Intl. Indoor Tennis Corp. / 1989	Marilyn Fernberger / Tournament Director	85,000
Philadelphia Marine Trade Assn. / 1990	Thomas P. Kelly / President	86,000
Philadelphia Conven. & Visitors Bureau / 1991	Thomas Muldoon / President	170,081
	Andrew Tod / Vice President	133,747
Poynter Institute for Media Studies / 1991	Robert J. Haiman / President	163,481
	Roy Peter Clark / Dean	101,907
Princeton University Press / 1990	Walter H. Lippincott / Resident Agent and Secretary	131,212
Professional Golfers' Assn. (PGA) / 1990	Jim L. Awtrey / Executive Director	235,072
Public/Private Ventures / 1990	Michael A. Bailin / President	152,924
Research Triangle Institute / 1990	F.T. Wooten / President	156,474
Robert Morris Associates / 1991	Clarance R. Reed / Executive Vice President	160,921
Society of Automotive Engineers / 1990	Max E. Rumbaugh Jr. / Vice President	175,491
Southeastern Universities Res. Assn. / 1991	William A. Wallenmeyer / President	155,000
Southwest Research Institute / 1991	M. Goland / President	459,695
SRI International / 1991	James J. Tietjen / President	556,148
	Paul J. Jorgensen / Executive Vice President	469,244
	Osamu Hirose / Regional Vice President/Japan	362,859
Sugar Association / 1991	Charles D. Shamel / President	209,146
Teachers Insur. & Annu. Assn. Amer. / 1990	J. Daniel Lee / Executive Vice President	681,063
	John H. Biggs / President	533,052
Underwriters Laboratories Inc. / 1990	G.T. Castino / President	197,528
United Nations Development Corp. / 1991	Thomas Appleby / President	165,769
Universities Res. Assn. (Fermi Lab) / 1991	John S. Toll / President	231,893
University Corp. for Atmospheric Res. / 1990	Richard A. Anthes / President	175,125
University of Pennsylvania Press / 1990	Thomas Rotell / Director	153,458
U.S. Olympic Comm. / 1990	Harvey Schiller / Executive Director	253,635
	Baaron Pittenger / Executive Director	240,173
Wistar Institute / 1990	Hilary Koprowski / Director/Professor	206,000
Woods Hole Oceanographic Inst. / 1990	Craig E. Dorman / Director	134,520

* Compensation includes severance or lump-sum retirement benefit.
[1] Includes income from Pew Charitable Trusts and Glenmede Trust Co.

When University of Pittsburgh president Wesley W. Posvar
retired in 1991, he received a compensation package worth
$3.3 million, plus a pension of $201,600 a year. Following a
public outcry, the pension was reduced to $141,600 a year.
∎ Charities and other nonprofits have given millions of dollars in low-interest or no-interest loans to executives to buy
houses, redecorate residences, join country clubs, or pay for
children's schooling. In 1991, UCLA chancellor Charles E.
Young received $995,000 in low-interest loans to buy a $1.17
million house thirty-five miles from campus.
∎ Dozens of universities and hospitals provided free housing,
food and liquor, domestic help, fresh-cut flowers, vacation
junkets, and gifts to executives. New England Medical Center in Boston spent more than $70,000 in 1991 redecorating
its president's office.
∎ Executives of many large nonprofits were provided luxury
cars or generous auto allowances. An executive of the
J. Paul Getty Trust drove a $36,000 Jaguar, the president of
the National Academy of Sciences was chauffeured around
Washington in a luxury car, and the TMCA Foundation in
Boston spent $986,643 on auto leases for its doctors.
∎ Entertaining by executives was a big expense at many nonprofits. Between 1986 and 1990, Blue Cross of Western
Pennsylvania spent $377,101 to rent a skybox at Three
Rivers Stadium, buy tickets to sporting events, and pay
country-club dues for top executives. Ratepayers picked up
the tab.
∎ Seminars, conferences, and staff development meetings—
sometimes in exotic places—have become routine items.
The Devereux Foundation in Devon, Pennsylvania, flew
thirty executives to Key West for a week of planning and
rest, including a catered sunset yacht cruise. Cost exclud-
ing airfare: $9,000.
Pay and perks like these have grown over the last two decades as nonprofit institutions have grown—at a rate four times
the rest of the economy. Nonprofits now control assets worth at
least $850 billion.
The growth in nonprofits has created more than three million
jobs. That has helped ease the impact of the decline of American industry and has elevated incomes of many workers, particularly in health care. But the growth came at a price. This

economic transformation has cost federal, state, and local governments—ultimately, taxpayers—more than $36 billion a year in lost taxes.

All this has occurred largely without notice, forethought, or debate over the implications for the economy or public policy. And executive compensation at nonprofits *does* have public policy implications.

Take health care. At a time when thirty-seven million Americans cannot afford health insurance, more than one thousand executives and doctors at nonprofit hospitals and insurance plans were paid salaries ranging from $200,000 to $1.2 million.

"A lot of people are being priced out of health-care coverage. What people get paid—whether it's physicians or administrators of hospitals or CEOs of insurance companies—is a factor," said Ron Pollack, executive director of Families USA, a Washington advocacy group. "Somebody has to foot the bill for these salaries, and that somebody is you and me."

At for-profit companies, such expenses come out of earnings of shareholders, who, theoretically at least, can object. In nonprofit organizations, there is often little oversight.

"The problem with nonprofits is that there are no shareholders to serve as a brake. There's no one there unless there is a responsible board of directors or, at last resort, the IRS," IRS executive Jay Rotz said in 1992.

Until recently, the Internal Revenue Service paid little demonstrable attention to the extraordinary increases in executive pay packages among large nonprofit groups. IRS officials now say they have begun to scrutinize executive salaries in their audits of Form 990s, the annual statements each nonprofit must file with the IRS. Yet the agency has not conducted a detailed study of executive compensation in tax-exempt groups.

By its own admission, the IRS is reluctant to challenge big salaries unless it can prove that executives are unfairly using their positions to enrich themselves. The agency's top regulator of nonprofits acknowledges that the whole salary area "is very gray." One reason: There are no established guidelines. Another: Inadequate staffing. IRS audits of tax-exempt groups declined by half in the last decade.

The IRS has received little guidance from Congress. There has not been a major congressional hearing on executive pay of any sort in a quarter-century, let alone on what IRS should consider appropriate pay. State and local agencies have done little. Most are understaffed or lack the expertise and data to analyze nonprofits' pay. In short, whatever accountability does exist stems from the nonprofit institutions themselves. It is not always rigorous.

Many of the same board members who are expected to police the pay of nonprofit executives are themselves in business with their nonprofit organizations. Form 990s show hundreds of instances in which attorneys, accountants, financial advisers, and consultants sell their services to the nonprofits they help to direct.

For example, Graduate Hospital in Philadelphia has leased medical and office equipment from a company run by a board member; has hired management, consulting, and architectural services from other board members; and has contracted for TV services for patients and insurance coverage from still others. Hahnemann University Hospital in Philadelphia contracted with board members' companies to lease equipment, provide credit lines, operate food services, and provide telephone service, financial management, and computer information services.

A nonprofit business in Montgomery County, Pa., that develops retirement homes paid more than $4 million a year in fees to a management company owned by a member of the board. Richard S. Coons was both chairman of the board of the nonprofit Adult Communities Total Services and president of the for-profit Total Care Systems. In June 1990, the management company was sold for $10.3 million to a Kennett Square nursing home chain. Genesis Health Ventures obtained the right to be the "exclusive manager and developer" of the nonprofit's expanding group of retirement centers.

In each of these examples, officers of the nonprofits say the transactions were conducted at arm's length and were disclosed to other board members. It is impossible to say how often such business arrangements occur. Many nonprofits do not report instances of self-dealing or do not provide financial details. Or they conduct such transactions through subsidiaries and for-profit companies, outside the reach of disclosure rules.

"Trustees too often are on the board simply as fund-raisers, or worse yet, as vendors of legal, financial, construction, real estate, medical, and other services," Nancy B. Kane, a professor at the Harvard School of Public Health, recently testified before Congress.

Officials of large tax-exempt groups maintain that big salaries are not at odds with the special social mission of nonprofits or their privileged tax-exempt status. They offer four main arguments:

- Pay packages reflect increased duties. Today's executives have to deal with complex regulations, growing competitive pressures, and are managing larger staffs and budgets.
- Large nonprofit organizations now compete with private firms for executive talent. So they must offer competitive salaries, benefits, and perks if they are to attract managers of superior ability.
- Nonprofit executives travel in the same corporate circles as their for-profit counterparts and play a key role in fund-raising.
- Increasing numbers of executives move back and forth between nonprofit and for-profit organizations. As they do, differences in salaries tend to disappear.

Take John Gavin, who is paid $519,000 as chairman of the Century Council, a Los Angeles nonprofit funded by the liquor, beer, and wine companies to combat alcohol abuse and deflect criticism of the industry. Gavin has been a movie actor, Ronald Reagan's ambassador to Mexico, and a businessman.

"For a man of his stature, that is appropriate compensation," said Tom Ross, a senior vice-president of Hill & Knowlton, a public relations firm that represents the council.

It hasn't always been that way. Once, for-profit and nonprofit groups had very different missions and operated in very different ways. For-profit companies built markets and made money. Their managers took risks and were well paid—or fired—for their performance.

The purpose of not-for-profit groups was to provide important community services that would otherwise fall to government. Charities and nonprofits relied on contributions from the public and used the money to provide free services—what most Americans think of as charity. The tax exemption was granted in recognition of these services.

Today, many large nonprofits are indistinguishable from for-profit companies. They make millions of dollars in profits. They have millions of dollars in stocks, bonds, and other investments. And instead of relying on donations, they charge for their services, just like any other business, or are reimbursed by the government. Often they provide little or no charity.

"It used to be that the not-for-profit sector was its own world. You signed on after you got out of college, like if you joined the government, and you stayed there," said Robert C. Ochsner, director of compensation for Hay Associates, an employee benefits firm in Philadelphia. "There also was the realization that you never expected the same money you might earn in the for-profit world.

"Now we see people are crossing over. It's more common for people to go out of the not-for-profit to the for-profit sector, but it also works the other way around. Therefore, the markets are moving toward each other and the pay is catching up."

In some cases, the pay exceeds compensation of executives of commercial companies. A 1992 Hay survey found that the base pay of hospital executives was on average 2 percent higher than for executives at industrial firms of similar size.

Not everyone is part of this trend, or agrees with it. James Osborne, national commissioner for the Salvation Army, believes that the special mission of nonprofits separates them from profit-making companies. He is paid $53,000, including benefits, for overseeing an organization with a $1 billion budget.

"I really can't speak to why other organizations pay what they do. But I can tell you that people who come to work at the Salvation Army don't come into this work because they are looking for money. If that was our overwhelming passion in life, we would go elsewhere," Osborne said.

The rapid increase in compensation coincides with the growth in revenues and wealth of large tax-exempt groups in the last two decades, especially during the 1980s. The tax returns of nonprofit groups—they are required to file IRS Form 990s, even if they have no taxable income—show that pay packages for executives have far exceeded those of other workers as nonprofits have expanded, diversified their services, and become more commercial.

Consider a few examples, culled from tax returns in the last decade.

- In 1981, the president of Thomas Jefferson University in Philadelphia was paid $143,000. A decade later, the president received $399,196, including benefits and other allowances worth $109,196.

- In 1981, the president of Hahnemann University received $135,415. A decade later, the compensation was $493,898.
- In 1981, the president of Philadelphia's Children's Hospital received $141,165. In 1991, he was paid $433,200.

In the same period, the average salary of workers in Philadelphia rose from $16,231 to $26,456.

Now consider how these three hospitals grew between 1981 and 1991:

Thomas Jefferson University's revenues rose from $184 million to $550 million. Hahnemann University's revenues rose from $153 million to $619 million. Children's Hospital's rose from $66 million to $296 million.

"Many tax-exempt organizations are very large and complex. Whether the compensation package paid to the chief executive is reasonable would depend, I think, on looking at a number of factors," said Marcus S. Owens, director of the IRS's Exempt Organizations Technical Division. "What are the responsibilities? What are the decisions? Does it involve large amounts of money?"

"I see no problems in paying an executive a livable salary. In fact, I think you have to if you are going to run the business successfully—and a nonprofit is a business," said Pamela Rainey Lawler, founder of Philabundance, a Philadelphia charity that distributes free food to shelters and social agencies. "But there's a big difference between a livable salary and paying someone hundreds of thousands of dollars," she said. "Running a nonprofit is a matter of public trust. I'm afraid some people are getting removed from what they are doing. They're becoming insulated as managers and executives."

Rainey Lawler was executive director of Philabundance from 1984 until July 1992. Her salary never exceeded $25,000. She now serves as unpaid chairwoman.

There is little question that executives of nonprofit organizations shoulder more responsibilities than they once did. But comparing their salaries with executives in for-profit companies may not be the best way. Because one reason for the tax exemption is that the government is relieved of a burden, it might be more appropriate to compare these executives with top government officials. How do they fare?

In 1990, Secretary of State James A. Baker was paid $99,500. The chief justice of the United States, William H. Rehnquist, received $124,000. And in 1992, Philadelphia mayor Edward G. Rendell earned $104,500.

By comparison, the *lowest* paid executive of a nonprofit hospital in Philadelphia and its Pennsylvania suburbs received $98,000 in 1990. Only eight hospital executives were paid *less* than Rehnquist; forty were paid more.

Or apply the president's test. As chief executive of the United States, Bill Clinton is paid a salary of $200,000, plus $50,000 in expenses. The president also gets chauffeur service, housing, maid and valet, personal security, and extensive travel, at no charge.

Still, compared with many nonprofit executives whose pay and perks were listed on tax returns from 1989 to 1991, the president's compensation seems modest. For example:

- Richard Schweiker received a top salary of $61,000 a year as a United States senator from Pennsylvania in 1980. These days, as president of the nonprofit American Council of Life Insurance, a lobbying group, Schweiker collects $716,000 in salary and benefits—more than 3½ times the president's salary.
- Gilbert M. Grosvenor, president of the National Geographic Society, received $419,691 in salary and benefits.
- Peter J. Liacouras, president of Temple University in Philadelphia, received $407,059 in salary and benefits in 1991, including a $16,000 housing stipend. He is one of the highest-paid university presidents in the nation.
- James S. Todd, executive vice-president of the American Medical Association, received pay and benefits totaling $528,496.
- Cathleen Black, former president of *USA Today*, received $600,000 as executive director of the American Newspaper Publishers Association, a tax-exempt trade and lobbying group. The publishers also gave Black $300,000 for stock rights she forfeited when she left *USA Today*.
- William W. Whaley, a division president at Children's Television Workshop, producers of "Sesame Street," was paid $671,221.
- Jack Valenti, president of the Motion Picture Association of America, was paid $776,689.

- John W. Rowe, president of New York's Mt. Sinai Hospital and two affiliates, received $893,385.

At least one thousand employees of nonprofit organizations received more than the president of the United States. Two hundred collected at least twice as much as the president.

Then there's the nonprofit millionaires' club. NFL commissioner Paul Tagliabue was paid $1,511,731 in salary and benefits in 1991. His predecessor, Pete Rozelle, was paid $2,937,344 by the NFL in 1990. Rozelle resigned as commissioner in 1989, but according to the league's tax return, he served as "commissioner consultant" in 1990. He received $830,000 in 1991 and $710,000 in 1992.

In 1990, Walter M. Cabot earned $1,486,446 working for an investment house—a private, tax-exempt investment house. Cabot was president of Harvard Management Company, which occupies the entire fifteenth floor of the Federal Reserve's office tower in Boston's financial district. The company describes its charitable purpose as "providing investment research, advice, counsel, and management" to Harvard University. Cabot has since left the company.

Two other Harvard Management employees made more than $1 million. In 1989, Michael Eisenson and Scott Sperling were each paid $1,066,042. They ran Aeneas Group, a subsidiary that invests in real estate, start-up companies, and corporate takeovers.

The New York banking and insurance scene also provided several million-dollar nonprofit executives. In 1990, Clifton R. Wharton, Jr., was paid $1,283,650 as chairman and chief executive officer of Teachers Insurance & Annuity Association and the College Retirement Equity Fund. James S. Martin, chairman of the retirement fund's finance committee, received $1,068,529.

Formed in 1918 to pool pension contributions of university and college teachers, TIAA-CREF today is the world's largest pension fund, with assets of $100 billion. Records show the two companies paid more than $30 million to 167 senior managers in 1990. Thirty-seven executives were paid $200,000 or more, including four who made between $500,000 and $1 million.

Not far from TIAA-CREF's Manhattan offices is the headquarters of Mutual of America Life Insurance Company, a tax-exempt insurer with nearly $5 billion in assets. In 1991, Mutual's chairman and chief executive officer, William J. Flynn, was paid $1,058,702.

Another nonprofit millionaire: Paul A. Marks, a physician who is president and chief executive officer of Memorial Sloan-Kettering Cancer Center in New York and its affiliates. In 1991, Marks was paid more than $1 million in salary and benefits. In 1988, when Marks became the hospital's president, he got a $1 million "signing bonus" in return for a pledge to remain through 1994, it was reported.

How does the IRS's Owens explain the phenomenon of nonprofit millionaire? "Luckily, I don't have to," he said. "What our auditors would look at is how large is the tax-exempt organization, how much responsibility is involved. Is it a true job?"

Directors of some tax-exempt groups also receive large sums of money—another indication of how nonprofits have changed. Board members used to be called trustees and served a basic role: They were guardians of a community asset, entrusted with the responsibility of ensuring a charity's integrity. Today, many large nonprofits refer to their governing bodies as boards of directors, just as commercial businesses do. And like directors of publicly held companies, these board members are paid to attend meetings. They often are provided with perks of office.

The financial arrangements are often murky. What details do get out often are buried in the back pages of the tax returns. These show that nonprofits not only match private companies when it comes to directors' pay, they occasionally exceed it. Consider the Howard Hughes Medical Institute. In 1990, the research facility in Bethesda, Maryland, gave nine directors $335,002 in trustees fees—an average of $37,222 each.

In 1990, the American College of Physicians, based in Philadelphia, spent $958,077 on directors' fees and expenses. The largest fee, $41,500, was paid to Dr. Eugene A. Hildreth of Reading, Pennsylvania, chairman of the board of regents. On the group's Form 990, where a description of each board member's activities is required, the entry for Hildreth and his colleagues was identical: "minimal time."

"That's a mistake," said Dr. John Ball, executive vice-president. "Many of our trustees devote a substantial amount of time. These fees are a way of compensating them for their lost practice time."

Mutual of America, the New York nonprofit insurance and pension company, paid its directors $228,950 in 1991. The highest paid: William Aramony, former head of United Way. He got $31,000 to attend eight meetings, an average of $3,875 a meeting.

Aramony has been a director of Mutual of America since the early 1970s. During that time, the insurance company sold millions of dollars worth of services to various United Way groups around the country.

The John S. and James L. Knight Foundation, a tax-exempt organization created by the Knight brothers, who were executives of Knight Newspapers (now Knight-Ridder, corporate parent of *The Philadelphia Inquirer*), paid its trustees between $1,500 and $19,500 in 1991. The average: $10,750.

The Gannett Foundation, set up by the nation's largest newspaper group and later renamed The Freedom Forum, paid its part-time trustees between $8,333 and $98,833 in 1992. The average: $55,657.

By comparison, the average compensation for outside directors of the 150 largest industrial companies was $39,724, according to a 1991 survey by Hewitt Associates.

Officials say they pay directors in recognition of their growing responsibilities and workloads. "I think almost every large foundation board pays its trustees," said Steven A. Schroeder, president of the Robert Wood Johnson Foundation in Princeton. It "allows people who don't have great wealth to be able to do it," Schroeder said.

In fact, boards of most large foundations and nonprofits rarely include people who aren't wealthy, well known in the business community, or have some other connection to the organization, an analysis of board memberships shows.

Schroeder acknowledged that his and many other boards often do not include representatives of the public. "If you ask me how many paupers are on the board, I would tell you none. One of the things that happens is that boards often get set up to represent families or friends [of the original benefactor]. Friends of rich people tend to be rich people," he said.

These days, salary is only one part of executives' compensation. In 1991, half of all nonprofit hospitals in America—about sixteen hundred hospitals—paid executives cash bonuses, according to a Hay Associates survey. The bonuses accounted for about one-quarter of total compensation.

Take Larry L. Mathis, president and chief executive officer of the Methodist Hospital in Houston. In 1992, he was paid a bonus of $138,555. Mathis's bonus accounted for 24 percent of his $584,930 in total compensation.

Nonprofit executives and benefits consultants say there is nothing wrong with tying an executive's pay to financial performance. It's a responsible way to achieve a variety of goals, they say.

The practice does raise questions about the motivation of executives, and it blurs the lines between nonprofit and for-profit organizations, others say. Too strong an emphasis on financial performance could diminish the very services for which a tax exemption was granted, these critics say.

Indeed, the use of bonuses has been singled out in several lawsuits challenging the tax-exempt status of a nonprofit organization. "Incentives based on profit are directly contradictory to a lack of profit motive," Erie County Common Pleas judge George Levin wrote in a May 1990 case involving Hamot Health Systems in Erie, Pennsylvania.

"Each executive who participates in these benefits knows that he or she will receive more money if the institution generates more profits. . . . How is such a payment possible without a private profit motive?"

Court records in the Hamot case show that President Dana Lundquist received incentive pay of $41,557 in 1988 and $37,980 in 1989. That was in addition to salary of $189,900 in 1988 and $206,991 in 1989. Lundquist earned about $275,000 in 1991, a spokeswoman said. Lundquist resigned from Hamot in 1992.

Bonuses come in all shapes and sizes. In 1989, Dr. Buris Boshell, part-time executive director of the Diabetes Trust Fund in Birmingham, Alabama, was paid a one-time bonus of $300,000, in addition to his $100,000 salary. A note attached to the group's 1989 tax return states that the trustees "voted the executive director a special one-time bonus in the amount of $300,000 for his past services to the trust fund. This equates to a salary of about $20,000 per year for the first fifteen years of the trust fund, when the executive director served without compensation."

In an interview, Boshell said the trustees had given him the bonus when he took early retirement because his previous employer closed part of a diabetes clinic he ran at the University of Alabama at Birmingham. "My board went to the university and explained that [early retirement] certainly would create financial distress for me," he said. "They asked for a golden parachute for me, and, to make a long story short, the university said 'no.' The board then decided that I should get $300,000 for the many, many years I had put into the clinic." Today, Boshell runs a diabetes clinic for another Birmingham hospital and continues to earn $100,000 as a part-time executive director of the trust fund.

The nonprofit Devereux Foundation in Devon, Pa., also has spent tens of thousands of dollars a year on executive bonuses based in part on financial performance. Court records and interviews show that the foundation has paid senior executives cash bonuses ranging from $6,000 to $50,000. The largest went to Devereux president Ronald P. Burd, who received a $50,000 bonus in 1991, and total compensation of $281,622. Burd's pay package included a $6,000 car allowance.

In 1992, Burd's bonus fell to about $42,000. Devereux's trustees have since decided to eliminate bonuses based on financial incentives. "Quite frankly, I don't think it motivated our already really dedicated staff," Burd said. Asked about the foundation's Key West outing and yachting cruise for thirty executives, Burd said it was "cheaper and also more productive" to hold the meeting in Key West than in the Philadelphia area.

Leaving a nonprofit also can be highly profitable. When University of Pittsburgh president Wesley Posvar announced his retirement in 1991, following nearly a quarter-century at the school, it was disclosed that he would receive a $3.3 million annuity, an annual pension of $201,600, lifetime health coverage, and use of a university office.

Some state legislators in Harrisburg cried foul. After all, Pitt was a nonprofit organization, not a *Fortune* 500 company, they complained. Such a generous retirement package sent the wrong message.

Pitt officials responded that Posvar had accepted a salary of

$45,000 in 1967 when he arrived at the school, which was then heavily in debt. Under Posvar, Pitt had not only rebounded, it had thrived, they said.

Posvar eventually agreed to accept an annual pension of $141,600 and to repay low-interest mortgages from the university totaling $740,000. He said his retirement package was comparable to corporate executives'. Not to mention those of other university executives.

In 1992, the University of California voted its outgoing president, David Gardner, a lump-sum retirement of $797,000, plus an annual pension of $130,000. Gardner, who also received generous housing loans, travel arrangements, and other perks, was president of the university ten years.

Transcripts of the board meeting at which Gardner's retirement package was voted show that some of the regents were worried about the potential for negative publicity. "If the legislature gets hold of this . . . when we're increasing fees . . . it's very difficult to reconcile," regent Frank Clark said.

Large nonprofits often supplement income of key executives by lending them money—sometimes at little or no interest. The IRS views such loans as part of executives' total compensation. It does not prohibit interest-free or below-market loans but takes them into account in considering whether compensation is excessive. "We put it all out there on the scale of reasonableness and see if it balances," Owens said.

The Philadelphia Inquirer identified more than two hundred loans to executives, totaling nearly $20 million, made by charities and other nonprofit groups in the years 1989 through 1992. Including mortgage loans made by universities to faculty members, the value of loans exceeded $250 million.

The majority were to buy houses. For instance, in 1990, Georgetown University lent its vice-president for urban affairs, Samuel Harvey, $332,304 to buy a house. The thirty-year mortgage was at 9.63 percent interest.

Two years earlier, the university made two loans totaling $751,880 to John Griffith, executive vice-president of the university's medical center, to buy a residence. One loan for $107,500 carried a 5 percent interest rate. The other was a no-interest loan for $644,380. In all, Georgetown listed $1,631,792 in loans to three senior officers in its 1990 IRS filing.

John Silber, president of Boston University, received three loans totaling $638,921 in the mid-1980s. One, for $138,921, was to buy a house and was interest-free, according to the university's tax return. The loan was issued April 15, 1983, and Silber did not have to begin making monthly payments of $2,315 until January 1992.

Another nonprofit organization that has made mortgage loans to officers and key employees is the National Collegiate Athletic Association, based in Overland Park, Kansas. Tax returns for 1990 listed $1,451,015 in outstanding loans to officers and employees. The single largest NCAA borrower was Executive Director Richard D. Schultz, who owed $247,016 on a mortgage loan. Schultz's salary in 1990 was $328,438.

The NCAA, which lists its exempt purpose as an educational association, oversees the sports programs of more than one thousand universities and colleges. One of its roles is investigating schools for violations of NCAA rules. In September 1992, it suspended Demetrius DuBose, an All-America linebacker at Notre Dame, for two games. DuBose's sin: accepting a $600 loan from two football boosters.

Let's do all we can to relieve childhood suffering," said a recent fund-raising plea from former United States surgeon general C. Everett Koop on behalf of Children's Hospital of Philadelphia. "It costs over $267 million to run this hospital every year," another mailing said. "We can meet these expenses only with the support of caring, compassionate people. And that is why I hope you'll help us by making a donation of $20, $25, $50, or even $100 today."

Where does the money go? In 1987, $600,000 was used by Children's Hospital's president Edmond Notebaert to purchase a $550,000 house in Chester County. The money came in the form of a no-interest cash loan made to Notebaert by the tax-exempt Children's Hospital Foundation.

Most charities that make loans to their officers describe them in their tax returns, as required by the IRS. Children's officials did not spell out terms of the Notebaert loan in their tax returns for the years 1987 through 1990. There was no record made of the interest rate, the length of the loan, or how it was secured. The only reference to the loan came in response to a form question about lending of money. There, hospital officials wrote: "mortgage loan to president."

When first asked about the loan in December 1991, Notebaert responded, "We think we have provided the necessary disclosure and would prefer not to offer any more information." Notebaert declined several other requests for comment. Property records in Chester County show that on July 31, 1987, he purchased a house on 3.4 acres in East Goshen Township. That day, Notebaert obtained a ten-year mortgage loan for $600,000 on the property from the tax-exempt Children's Hospital Foundation.

In March 1992, Children's officials reversed themselves and filed a schedule with a tax return for fiscal year 1991 disclosing the terms of the loan. The return filed by The Children's Hospital Foundation described the loan as: to "facilitate relocation to Philadelphia for employment." Notebaert is paying $2,500 a month on the loan, with the balance due August 31, 1997. Under "interest rate," the return notes: 0%.

CHAPTER 7

Cheap money, for nonprofits only

This is a lesson in how to buy and sell nursing homes and make millions of dollars in profits while using someone else's money.

First, negotiate a deal with a financially troubled company to buy a chain of nursing homes. Next, quickly arrange to sell the nursing homes to a nonprofit organization set up by a business associate. It's okay if the nonprofit doesn't have any money or assets and has been inactive for a year or two. Before you sell, raise the price by $6.5 million; that's your gross profit.

As part of the deal, negotiate contracts to manage the nursing homes, to make renovations, and to collect patient bills—contracts potentially worth up to $5 million. Now the critical part. To pull all this off, you'll need more than $80 million. That's where the taxpayers come in.

Thanks to Congress, there's a vast pool of cheap money available if you're a nonprofit organization. It's called tax-exempt bonds. All you have to do is persuade a public authority to issue tax-exempt bonds for the nonprofit buyers to finance the purchase. And your associates get to serve as underwriters in the bond sale, earning $8 million in fees.

Sound too good to be true? It's true.

Bruce Hayne Whitehead, a former Texas bank examiner turned

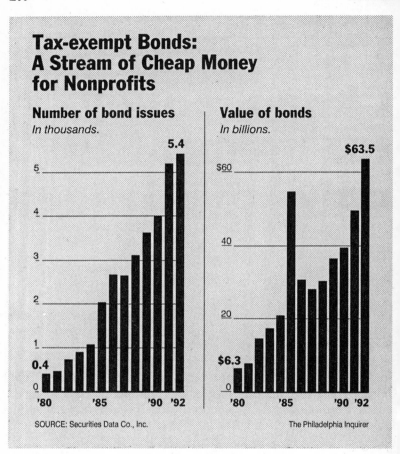

Tax-exempt Bonds: A Stream of Cheap Money for Nonprofits

Number of bond issues
In thousands.

Value of bonds
In billions.

SOURCE: Securities Data Co., Inc.

The Philadelphia Inquirer

mergers-and-acquisition specialist, and associates arranged such a deal in 1989. They got $86 million to finance a two-step transaction in which they bought and sold forty-five Iowa nursing homes. Fueling Whitehead's deal was one of the fastest-growing methods of financing in the nation: tax-exempt bonds.

Hospitals, nursing homes, colleges, and other nonprofit organizations can tap into this seemingly endless stream of cash. Say a nonprofit sells low-interest bonds through a public authority. The cost of borrowing millions of dollars might be only 7 percent a year for decades, compared with a commercial rate of 10 percent.

The lower interest rates are meant to enable charitable organizations to fund worthy projects. And investors get a break by not having to pay taxes on the interest income they earn on these bonds. Taxpayers, of course, subsidize all this.

This low-interest financing is merely one of the tax breaks that have boosted the tremendous growth of nonprofit organizations in the last two decades. The cost in lost taxes is well over $36 billion a year. Tax-exempt bonds are a key part of that tax-free economy.

The United States Treasury estimates that about $2 billion is lost each year in federal taxes on interest income from these bonds. This method of taxpayer-subsidized financing was made available to charities and other nonprofit organizations by Congress so they could build hospitals and colleges or fill other socially beneficial needs.

In practice, though, tax-exempt bonds often are used for less high-minded purposes—such as buying and selling real estate, financing mergers, building exclusive retirement communities, and taking taxpaying businesses off the tax rolls. Which gets back to Bruce Hayne Whitehead and his $86 million nursing-home deal.

The fallout from that transaction is still being felt across forty Iowa communities. In towns like Creston, in sparsely populated Union County, the sale resulted in a bitter lawsuit over the payment of property taxes by the local nursing home, Creston Manor.

In 1990, the new owners, Mercy Health Initiatives, asked county officials to exempt the nursing home from paying $30,000 a year in property taxes. The reason: They were a nonprofit organization.

County Tax Assessor A.D. Paxton balked. "To my knowledge, they weren't doing anything different up there than before, when they were owned by Beverly Enterprises," the for-profit firm that sold the nursing home, Paxton said in an interview. A county tax board upheld Paxton's ruling. The nonprofit, which by then had changed its name to Care Initiatives, filed suit.

In September 1991, after a week-long trial, Iowa district judge Gene L. Needles issued a stinging twenty-one-page decision in favor of the tax board and Paxton. "Care Initiatives is a 'shell' nonprofit corporation used by Bruce H. Whitehead and the bond underwriters to obtain financing necessary to enable them to make millions of dollars of excessive profits," Needles wrote.

"Care Initiatives serves no legitimate purpose and was used primarily to obtain tax-exempt financing, shield the parties using the facilities from liabilities and obligations as owners, and to evade the payment of property taxes," Needles went on. "The property is not being used by a charitable institution or organization."

Whitehead declined to be interviewed. In a brief telephone conversation, he said he had "taken substantial financial risks" in the Iowa transaction and had earned his profits. In a deposition, he said he had put more than $1 million of his own money into the deal.

Attorneys for Care Initiatives have appealed Judge Needles's decision to the Iowa Supreme Court, where the case is pending. The nonprofit lost a similar case in another Iowa county.

"I think these guys thought they could come up here from Texas and roll all over us hicks from Iowa," Paxton said. Since the judge's ruling, tax assessors in other Iowa counties are poised to revoke the tax exemptions of Care Initiatives' thirty-eight other homes, Paxton said. "If the Supreme Court upholds our case, you can expect the others to follow suit."

E ach day, hundreds of quasi-public agencies and state governments issue tax-exempt bond offerings for nonprofit groups. These authorities don't actually borrow the money. They merely serve as conduits for the real borrower—the hospital, college, or nonprofit institution that runs the project once it is built and is responsible for paying back the debt.

Instead of turning to private money markets, where they would have to pay higher commercial interest rates on the money they borrow, nonprofit groups are able to turn to their own private market for raising capital. The lower financing costs can result in savings of millions of dollars in interest.

It is a growing business, this market for taxpayer-subsidized bonds. Throughout America, in communities so small they don't have a town hall to cities the size of Philadelphia, tax-exempt bonds have become one of the most favored forms of financing.

In 1980, the volume of tax-exempt bonds sold by nonprofit organizations was more than $6 billion. In 1992, it was almost $64 billion. Between 1980 and 1992, the value of bonds issued for nonprofits grew an average 21 percent a year—compared with 13 percent for other types of bonds issued by public authorities, such as those to finance water and sewer systems.

There are several reasons for the rapid growth. One is that nonprofit organizations, just like home owners in the last few years, refinanced existing bonds to cash in on lower interest rates. Another is that, over time, many bond authorities came to view their role as an economic development agency, not as a protector of the public purse deciding whether a project deserved taxpayer-subsidized money. If the numbers added up, and a proposal wasn't especially risky, the authority pushed it through, rarely questioning whether it was really needed.

In May 1992, for instance, the Hospitals Authority of Philadelphia boasted in a letter about being named the number-one issuer of tax-exempt bonds. "A first for Philadelphia," the letter began. "I wish to share with you a significant community accomplishment. . . . We have just learned that the Philadelphia Hospitals Authority has been ranked the number-one health-care issuer in the United States. The figure of $360 million invested by private investors shows considerable confidence in Philadelphia.

"Our city is a major health-care center, and we are growing," authority president Donald A. Cramp wrote. "Philadelphia has seen more health-care financing activity than many large states— combined!"

Cramp's enthusiasm notwithstanding, the taxpayers of Philadelphia pay a price for all this development. The city is consistently ranked among the most expensive in the nation for hospital and health services. A growing portion of patient bills goes to pay for the debt on all this new construction. And more tax-exempt property falls off the city tax rolls.

"Authorities play the role both of lenders and as economic developers," said John Van Gorkom, president of the National Council of Health Finance Authorities. "We clearly are economic developers."

Still another explanation for the growth is the number of authorities. In about half the states, a single agency or authority acts as the conduit for bonds. In other states, there are dozens of authorities. In New Jersey, for example, tax-exempt bonds are issued either by the Economic Development Authority or the New Jersey Health Care Facilities Finance Authority.

By contrast, Pennsylvania has 103 authorities that issue bonds only on behalf of hospitals, colleges, and nursing homes. (And that does not include another 2,137 municipal and county authorities in Pennsylvania that issue bonds for *other* public purposes, such as parking garages and sewers.)

For tax-exempt bonds for nonprofit organizations, Pennsylvania has an average of nearly two authorities per county. Why so many? One explanation is politics.

In Pennsylvania, distributing lucrative bond-underwriting work to favored law firms, investment bankers, financial advisers, and other consultants has long been a part of county politics. Those who get the work often contribute to political campaigns.

Some Pennsylvania bonding authorities are so small they don't even have offices. When a bond issue is needed, politicians call up an underwriter and lawyers; the process essentially takes place by mail.

Others are known as "captive authorities," created by the nonprofit organization selling the bonds, housed in an office of the nonprofit, and existing only to sell its bonds.

Often authorities compete to sell bonds. And it is not unusual for a nonprofit that gets rejected by one authority to turn to another authority to issue its bonds.

In Pennsylvania, the Department of Community Affairs is responsible for tracking activities of authorities. But officials concede that they have little control over these many authorities, let alone regulate them.

Oversight is so loose that many authorities don't bother to send copies of their annual report and audited financial statement to the state government in Harrisburg, as required by law. "Largely speaking, they're pretty much on their own," said Robert B. Evans, municipal consultant in the Pennsylvania Department of Community Affairs. "No state agency in any sense is really controlling the authorities. They establish their own rules, their own rates," Evans said.

Local control comes at a price. Bond defaults are much more likely to involve bonds issued by smaller authorities than those issued by states with single authorities, industry data show.

In 1992, the number of defaults associated with local authorities was twenty times greater than defaults associated with state authorities, according to data from the Bond Investors Association. There were eighteen bond defaults, with a value of

$255 million, that had been issued by state authorities. There were 360, for more than $2 billion, issued by local authorities. Investors, of course, got stuck.

"I think the numbers speak for themselves," Van Gorkom said. "I can't speculate. But I will say I think you need an active staff and authority, and on the local level that's not always the case."

Richard Lehmann, president of the Bond Investors Association, which tracks bond defaults, puts it more bluntly. "The reason for the difference in the default rates is quite simply that the larger authorities at the state or city level have a greater level of expertise and due diligence than smaller, local authorities that may issue bonds only once a year, or less than that.

"There's also more influence at the local level," he said. "Quite frankly, it's kind of an old buddy network, where the local authority issuing the bonds is made up of all local residents who know little or nothing about bonds, but know a lot more about pleasing their old buddies."

Many of the defaulted bonds were unrated by credit agencies, such as Moody's and Standard & Poor's. Many of the defaults have involved nursing home and retirement centers. Between 1980 and 1992, a total of 280 such bonds ended in default, worth more than $2 billion, the Bond Investors Association said.

Even in cases where the IRS suspects abuses, there is little it can do. The IRS could rescind the tax break investors get. But that would "only punish the innocent party in the transaction," said Marcus S. Owens, director of the IRS's Exempt Organizations Technical Division, which oversees nonprofits. It would not penalize the nonprofit, underwriters, or consultants who sold the bonds.

"There is no intermediate sanction. It would be useful to have a penalty or sanction that would address the problem," he said. Only Congress can grant such a penalty, and it has not. In the meantime, IRS attorneys are negotiating more and more voluntary agreements with organizations when it believes there have been violations. And it is informing newly formed nonprofits that they may not use tax-exempt financing without prior approval from the service.

Owens said the IRS had twenty-seven audits under way that involve the use of tax-exempt bonds. Many of these cases came

Defaults on Tax-exempt Bonds for Retirement and Nursing Homes

Number of defaults

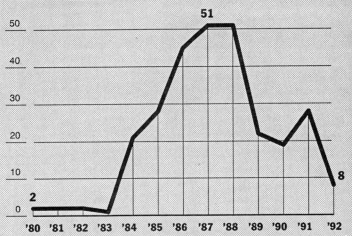

Value of bonds in default
In millions.

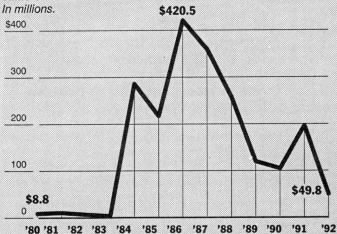

SOURCE: Bond Investors Association   The Philadelphia Inquirer

to the government's attention through public complaints, he said.

Of course, officials where the nonprofits are located have an alternative. If the bond deal involves a change of ownership, such as in the Iowa case, they can challenge or revoke the exemption for property taxes. It does not happen very often. When it does, sparks usually fly.

The tale of Care Initiatives begins with Bruce Whitehead, a Dallas financier who once offered to settle a dispute with the chairman of the Arkansas Finance Authority in the alley outside a meeting hall.

Asked to describe his business in a 1991 deposition, Whitehead responded that at one time or another, he had been involved in banking, construction, furniture and auto parts stores, a machine shop, an insurance agency, oil and gas, real estate, a fast-food franchise, apartments, retirement housing, an airplane charter company, and a firm for brokering and selling planes. "My principal day-to-day activity is working on mergers and acquisitions and financing," Whitehead testified at the Iowa trial.

A 1973 graduate of the University of Texas with a degree in finance and accounting, Whitehead started his career as a credit analyst with the Continental Bank in Houston, and shortly thereafter went to work for the Texas Banking Department as an assistant examiner. By the time he left in the late 1970s, he was senior examiner in charge of thirty-five banks in central Texas.

In 1984, Whitehead bought a bank in Amarillo and merged it with another local bank. That year, he also formed The Britwill Company, a management firm, and entered the nursing home business. He developed three nursing homes, which he later sold to a nonprofit corporation, Heartway III. The sale was financed with tax-exempt bonds.

One of the people involved in the Heartway III transaction was Terry Colip, an investment banker with whom Whitehead had done business since the mid-1980s. It was Colip, Whitehead later testified in the Iowa case, who first steered the Iowa deal his way.

According to Whitehead's deposition, Colip was approached by a Dallas broker looking to arrange a sale of nursing homes owned by the debt-laden Beverly Enterprises Corporation, the largest for-profit nursing-home chain in the nation. Colip, in turn, suggested that the broker take the package to Whitehead, "that he thought I'd be a good person to work on it," Whitehead testified.

The original package called for Whitehead to buy facilities in Nebraska, South Dakota, Arkansas, and Iowa. He wasn't interested in South Dakota and ran into problems in Arkansas, where a bond deal he thought he had negotiated collapsed after unfavorable publicity.

In Arkansas, the plan was for Whitehead to buy the nursing homes from Beverly and sell them to a tax-exempt organization—a nonprofit set up especially for the deal. After local politicians questioned the sale, the state authority turned down the Whitehead group.

"And at the time that you were turned down, did you tell the chairman of the Arkansas Finance Authority that you would like to go out in the alley and settle it with him?" Whitehead was asked at the 1991 trial before Judge Needles in Iowa.

"Yes sir, I sure did," Whitehead responded.

No fistfight took place. Whitehead continued to negotiate in Iowa, where the reception was friendlier.

In August 1989, Whitehead's company, Ventana Investments, bought forty-five nursing homes from Beverly Enterprises for $57 million, a figure that included a $10 million profit for the nursing home chain. At the same time, Ventana sold forty-one of the nursing homes to the nonprofit Mercy Health Initiatives— later renamed Care Initiatives—for $63.5 million, leaving Whitehead a gross profit of $6.5 million. Thus, in the span of about twenty-four hours, two separate corporations made a total profit of $16.5 million on the sale of forty-five nursing homes that one financial analyst described at the time as a "fire sale."

Financing for the two-step sale was arranged through the Iowa Finance Authority, which issued $86 million in tax-exempt bonds on behalf of Mercy Health Initiatives. The amount of bonds was sharply higher than the sale price for the nursing homes because it included about $20 million in underwriters' fees and other charges.

The underwriters were Terry Colip, Whitehead's old business associate, and Richard Young of the now-defunct investment banking firm Underwood Neuhaus. They were paid more than $8.5 million—or 9 percent of the offering.

Colip, his brother Gregory, and Young also were the incorporators of Mercy Health Initiatives, a Texas nonprofit that had been inactive since it was formed in 1988. They served as directors until shortly before the bond offering, court records and incorporation papers show.

Of the dual role played by Terry Colip and Richard Young, Judge Needles later wrote: "During this negotiation period, [Mercy Health Initiative's] board of directors consisted of the two bond underwriters, Terry Colip and Richard Young, who made millions of dollars from the transaction, and Terry Colip's brother, Greg Colip."

Whitehead testified that Mercy Health Initiatives and its successor, Care Initiatives, were operated independently by their respective boards of directors. Whitehead and his firms had no control over either, he said.

Needles offered a different view. "Bruce H. Whitehead, Ventana Investments and The Britwill Co. [Whitehead's nursing home management firm] exercised significant influence and control over Care Initiatives at the time of the acquisition . . ." he wrote. "Mr. Whitehead and The Britwill Co. continue to exert influence and control over Care Initiatives and its ongoing operations. . . . Only Britwill can sign checks. No board member or officer has check-signing authority or has ever signed a check or paid a bill."

The Britwill Company had negotiated a contract to run the Iowa nursing homes for Care Initiatives. Before the closing of the two-step transaction, the Colip brothers and Richard Young resigned from Care Initiatives and a new board was named. Terry Colip and Young remained as underwriters in the bond deal.

At the time, Care Initiatives was little more than a shell. It had no assets, charitable contributions, or sources of income. After the sale of the homes, its capitalization consisted entirely of debt—the $86 million bond issue.

"Care Initiatives was one of several inactive Internal Revenue Code 501(c)(3) corporations which Terry Colip, Richard Young, Bruce Whitehead, and Ventana Investments had organized or otherwise had available and which they considered

using as vehicles to obtain tax-exempt bond financing necessary to fund the acquisition transactions," Needles wrote.

Ted Chapler, who took over as executive director of the Iowa
Finance Authority after the transaction, said the agency's directors discussed the various relationships in a telephone conference call and were satisfied there were no problems. "The
various attorneys involved also reviewed those and decided
there was nothing contravening the law in those relationships,"
he said.

Chapler said the authority members viewed the bond offering
as a "good deal for Iowans. There was a discussion at the time
of what happens if it [the sale] doesn't go through. Homes will
be closed and rural Iowans will be kicked out, and the economic
base of those towns will be ruined," he recalled the members
saying.

Chapler said authorities such as his had little choice but to
issue tax-exempt bonds if the finances of the charitable organization appeared to be in order. "I don't offer it as an excuse, but
we were—and are—constrained by existing federal law. It does
not grant us a lot of latitude. As long as they complied with all
of the facets of the law allowing this type of activity, we had no
basis not to issue the bonds. In essence we're hamstrung by the
law," he said.

Paxton, the Union County tax assessor, wasn't feeling nearly
as generous. When he reviewed the application of Care Initiatives for a property-tax exemption for its Creston Manor Nursing Home, Paxton thought, "No way." Paxton said he concluded
that nothing had changed at Creston Manor except a desire to
be free of property taxes of about $30,000 a year: "I rejected
their application."

Attorneys for Care Initiatives appealed to a county board,
which upheld the assessor's ruling. A lawsuit was then filed,
leading to the July 1991 trial.

In the weeklong session, Whitehead testified that he had
taken a substantial financial risk. Without tax-exempt financing, he questioned whether the sale could have taken place.

Judge Needles wrote that the bond offering had left Care
Initiatives saddled with debt. He called the 9 percent underwriter fees "unreasonable and excessive." Combined with
Whitehead's gross profit of $6.5 million, "the two fees consti-
tute approximately 18 percent of the debt financing," he wrote.

"Such excessive costs are not normal or reasonable financing costs."

Attorneys for Care Initiatives dispute Needles's findings. In court papers appealing the decision, they said the relationship between Care Initiatives and Whitehead's companies "was at arm's length" and that the various fees were "fair and reasonable."

"[Needles] apparently believes that Bruce Whitehead engineered the sale of the Iowa facilities without any check against his own self-interest. The overwhelming weight of the evidence, however, shows that the transactions were carefully analyzed and thoroughly reviewed up front by all parties involved as well as their counsel," the attorneys wrote.

In April 1993, attorneys for Paxton and Care Initiatives made oral arguments before the state Supreme Court. A decision is pending.

In banking, there is an old saying that the only ones who can get loans are those who have money in the first place. At some bonding authorities, organizations that already have plenty of money often are the ones that get the breaks on tax-free bonds.

Take the New Jersey Economic Development Authority, a leading issuer of tax-exempt bonds. In 1991, the authority, an independent entity established by the state, approved $354 million in tax-exempt bonds.

Nearly $85 million of that went to nonprofit organizations. They ranged from Seeing Eye, the guide-dog trainer in Morris County, to the Institute of Management Accountants in Bergen County. By far, the largest nonprofit bond issue—one that accounted for almost one-third of the funding for nonprofits that year—was $25 million for the Lawrenceville School in Lawrence Township, Mercer County.

The private prep school wanted to add several buildings, including faculty housing, so it asked the state authority in July 1991 to approve $25 million in tax-exempt bonds. The cost of the projects was $30 million, of which 83 percent was financed through the bonds.

Lawrenceville is an exclusive school. Its fall 1993 tuition was $15,500, with another $3,400 for room and board, putting it well beyond the reach of most taxpayers. The school, grades eight through twelve, has about 750 students. Its 130-acre campus includes a private, nine-hole golf course, which is off the property-tax rolls.

According to its nonprofit tax filing, in the year ended June 30, 1990, Lawrenceville School had revenues of $27 million, with profit of $9.5 million. Its $78 million in securities and cash generated $5 million a year in dividends and interest.

Nevertheless, on its application to the Economic Development Authority, the school said that if it did not get tax-exempt financing, it would have to borrow money "on a higher taxable basis, which would lead to higher levels of tuition and a less competitive situation with respect to the schools that it competes with. There will also be less money available for financial aid, scholarships, and other programs."

Part of the $25 million was used to build new faculty housing on campus. At the same time, the tax-exempt school was loaning money from its own funds to faculty members at favorable rates.

Teachers aren't able to buy their own homes and build up equity because they must live on campus, said James T. Adams, Lawrenceville's assistant headmaster. So the school has made about $1.8 million in loans to faculty members for "retirement homes," according to Lawrenceville's IRS return.

The twenty-five-year mortgages, for up to $150,000, are made out of the school's endowment. The mortgages' interest rate is based on the rate of return the endowment earns.

Why did the New Jersey authority issue the bonds for Lawrenceville School? It was a major construction project during a deep recession in the construction industry, said Rose M. Smith, public affairs director of the authority. She said that the tax code allows such issues for nonprofit organizations like the Lawrenceville School. "There's no reason why the authority should not assist local nonprofit community organizations," Smith said.

According to the authority's annual report, its mission is "to retain and expand job opportunities, enlarge the tax base of the state and its local governments, and encourage economic growth and diversity."

The Lawrenceville School project temporarily employed about 690 construction workers. New, permanent jobs created by the expansion will total four, the school's bond application said.

As for enlarging the tax base, Lawrenceville School now has property valued at $73 million on the books at the Lawrence Township Assessor's Office. About 98 percent of that is exempt from property taxes—as the new construction will be. If tax-exempt Lawrenceville paid taxes on all its property, its real-estate tax bill would be $1.6 million a year.

Two years ago, municipal assessor William H. Hough tried to tax several houses the school had bought for faculty members. "I didn't want to put them on the exempt property list," he said.

The school took its challenge to the Mercer County Board of Taxation and "that was the end of that," he said. Hough said that because he has "been burned once," he won't try to collect property taxes on the faculty houses Lawrenceville has built on its campus with the bond money.

High on the list of projects borrowers have defaulted on are expensive retirement centers built with tax-exempt bonds. A 1991 report by the General Accounting Office took note of dramatic growth in the use of tax-exempt bonds to finance retirement centers.

In 1980, authorities issued $52 million in tax-exempt bonds for retirement projects, the GAO reported to Congress. In 1989, $614 million in bonds were issued for such projects—nearly twelve times as much.

In all, nonprofit organizations sold nearly $3 billion worth of tax-exempt bonds during the 1980s to build retirement centers. While other tax-exempt financing, such as industrial revenue bonds, had a default rate of about 1 percent, one of every five retirement centers built with tax-exempt bonds had defaulted, the GAO found. The GAO attributed this 20 percent default rate to the excessive debt of the retirement centers.

Unlike hospitals or other nonprofits that used reserves and donations to help finance new projects, the retirement centers had little, if any, equity of their own. Thus the heavy debt loads.

The GAO report also found that the majority of the retirement centers built with tax-exempt financing were too costly to be affordable to most elderly citizens. Only about one-quarter of the elderly could meet the entrance fees and monthly dues, the congressional agency found. Thus the taxpayer-provided bond subsidy benefited a small segment of society—wealthy elderly people.

A review by *The Philadelphia Inquirer* of the financial operations of Philadelphia-area nonprofit retirement centers financed in whole or in part with tax-exempt bonds showed that some offered reduced rates to a limited number of people. But charity cases were few.

At Dunwoody Village, a retirement center in Newtown Square, Pennsylvania, ten residents were considered charity cases out of a population of 360. The ten charity cases were supported by interest income generated by a $1.4 million trust.

Dunwoody sold $11 million worth of tax-exempt bonds in 1992 through the Delaware County Authority. Officials said proceeds from the offering would be used to demolish the William H. Dunwoody Home, a residence built in 1924 that had housed some residents. A modern nursing care unit would be added.

To get into the nonprofit home, a retiree must pay $53,000 for a single studio unit and up to $195,000 for a two-bedroom deluxe country house. In addition, annual service fees range from $16,824 to $37,248.

Many people finance their entrance fees by selling their family homes. To meet the monthly fees, a couple would have to have annual retirement income ranging from $28,000 to $62,000, according to information in Dunwoody's bond filing.

A consultant's study for Dunwoody by Arthur Andersen & Company showed that the nonprofit's primary market area includes such suburban Philadelphia Main Line communities as Bryn Mawr, Haverford, and Wayne. Even with such wealthy areas to draw from, Dunwoody was within the financial reach of about two of every ten residents seventy years and older in those areas.

Another local retirement center financed with tax-exempt bonds is White Horse Village, which is on eighty-three acres of a former thoroughbred horse farm in Delaware County. The four hundred retirees at White Horse Village live in cozy villas or apartments and dine in an elegant hall where jackets and ties are required. A branch of Fidelity Bank operates four afternoons a week. If a resident becomes ill, there's a full-service nursing home. Entrance fees at White Horse Village last year ranged from $78,400 for a studio apartment to $251,400 for a villa. Monthly fees run from $1,075 to $2,435.

Management of the nonprofit recommends that prospective members have retirement income of at least $30,000 a year to move into the smallest of the apartments. That financial requirement would exclude three-fourths of all households in the nation with people sixty-five or older, U.S. Census data show. The recommended annual income of $50,000 for an upscale villa would eliminate nine of ten older households.

The IRS counts the retirement center as a tax-exempt nonprofit. Started by a for-profit developer, the center was later completed with $48.5 million worth of tax-exempt bonds issued by the Delaware County Authority.

The proliferation of bonding authorities and the patchwork approach to government supervision often means that one agency doesn't know what another is doing. Take the American College, a nonprofit that offers correspondence courses in insurance and finance and seminars on its leafy campus just outside the center of Bryn Mawr.

In 1984, the Board of Assessment Appeals of Delaware County revoked the college's property-tax exemption, contending that it benefited the insurance industry more than the general public. The school appealed the ruling to Delaware County Court, Commonwealth Court, and finally to the Pennsylvania Supreme Court—losing at each stage.

The various courts ruled that the college did not meet the threshold required of charities to earn a property-tax exemption. As a result, the college was required to pay almost $2.5 million in back taxes.

That left American College with a problem—raising the money to pay the back taxes. American College not only figured out where to get the $2.5 million, but also another $3 million to pay off debts.

Thanks to the agreeable folks at the Delaware County Authority, American College was allowed to sell $5.5 million worth of tax-exempt bonds.

CHAPTER 8

Warehouses of wealth

When a new president took over the Robert Wood Johnson Foundation in Princeton, N.J., in 1990, he discovered a peculiar problem: Money was coming in much faster than it was going out.

The foundation's investment holdings, mostly in Johnson & Johnson Company stock and bonds, had tripled since 1981, to nearly $3 billion. While the assets had grown an average of 12 percent a year, grants had increased about 9 percent.

So in 1991 Steven A. Schroeder, the new president, decided the foundation needed to be more generous. And it was. It gave away $123 million. But even as it stepped up its giving that year, the Robert Wood Johnson Foundation managed to hand out no more than three cents in grants for every dollar in assets.

Many large foundations give away equally small proportions of their wealth. By distributing only the minimum required by law while their investments grow at a faster rate, tax-exempt foundations have become huge warehouses of wealth, where more money is stockpiled every year. And more and more of the nation's wealth is sucked out of the tax base—leaving taxpayers to pay a larger share.

It wasn't supposed to be this way: The tax laws, particularly the Tax Reform Act of 1969, were intended to require tax-

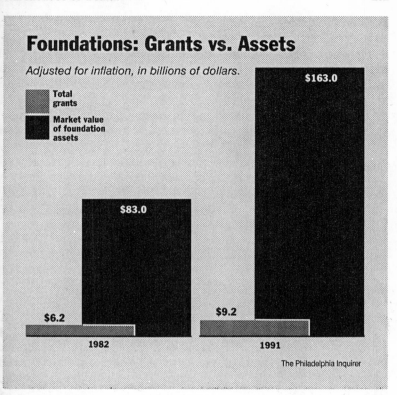

Foundations: Grants vs. Assets

Adjusted for inflation, in billions of dollars.

Total grants

Market value of foundation assets

$163.0

$83.0

$6.2

$9.2

1982

1991

The Philadelphia Inquirer

exempt foundations to give money away, not accumulate it. But a quarter-century after Congress studied the impact of foundations on the economy, more wealth is concentrated in a smaller number of foundations than ever before.

Today, foundations distribute about $9 billion a year in grants. There is no question that this results in a lot of good. The issue is whether the nation can afford to have so much wealth removed from the tax base.

These are the titans of the nonprofit world, that growing tax-exempt sector of the American economy that now controls property, cash, and investments worth at least $850 billion. About one-fifth of that wealth is controlled by foundations. Since 1975, their assets have swelled from $30 billion to $163 billion, a fivefold increase, according to the Foundation Center. Even after adjusting for inflation, their assets more than doubled, thanks to a booming stock market and favorable tax rules.

Foundations pay no income tax on this hoard of money. While businesses pay as much as 34 percent in income tax, a foundation typically pays only a 1 percent excise tax on income from its investments. If foundations were taxed at the full corporate rate on their income, which totaled nearly $9 billion in 1989, the federal government would have collected roughly $3 billion in taxes. Today, the estimated taxes would be about $4 billion.

Their proponents—mainly foundations themselves and those who benefit from their charity—say that private foundations are uniquely able to support innovation in social programs and research. Their opponents say they are tax shelters for the wealthy, a means by which a small, privileged class can continue to control billions of dollars while shifting the tax burden to people without substantial income.

"It has been much easier to make money than to spend it wisely," the late W.K. Kellogg, who established his own foundation in 1930, once said. His decades-old quote describes the position of many of the largest foundations today: Most appear to concentrate more on making money than on spending it—wisely or not.

The bulk of the $163 billion in foundation wealth is held by a few giants, under the control of self-perpetuating boards answerable only to themselves. Although there are thirty-three thousand foundations in the United States that make grants, the ten largest account for 20 percent of all assets and 12 percent of the grants. In the last two decades, control over this wealth has become even more concentrated. In 1972, the chairman of the House Banking Committee expressed alarm that 1 percent of foundations controlled 63 percent of all assets. Today, 1 percent controls 66 percent.

Operated like private banks or trusts, large foundations typically give away little more than the minimum required by law—the equivalent of 5 percent of their assets every year. When the 5 percent requirement was set by Congress seventeen years ago, it seemed like a fair amount. But since the run-up in assets during the 1980s, the adequacy of the 5 percent rule is less evident today.

Even that minimum payout is flexible: Five percent doesn't mean that 5 percent must be distributed each year to grant recipients. Allowable expenses, such as administrative costs of making the grants, can reduce it.

Take the foundation created by the late Robert Wood Johnson, who built a family business, Johnson & Johnson, into one of the biggest companies in the medical products industry. The Johnson Foundation focuses its interest on health-care issues.

In 1990, its assets totaled $2.9 billion, according to the foundation's annual report. However, a more narrowly drawn definition of assets permitted by the IRS showed it with $2.6 billion in assets on the foundation's 1990 tax return. A lower asset level means the 5 percent spending level for grants also is less. The $2.6 billion in assets meant the foundation had to show about $130 million in "qualifying distributions" on its tax return to escape paying a 2 percent excise tax as a penalty for not paying out enough.

Where did the $130 million go? Nearly $11 million was in administrative expenses, such as salaries for program managers; $3 million was paid in program-related investments, $4 million in other expenses, and nearly $46 million was in funds pledged but set aside for future grants. The balance—about $66 million, or the equivalent of 2.5 percent of the assets—actually went out in grants, according to the tax return.

Between 1990 and 1991, Schroeder's first year as president, assets grew by more than $1 billion, to a total of $4.1 billion—propelling the foundation from sixth largest to third largest in the nation.

In 1991, income and gains on the sale of securities totaled about $272 million. The year before, they totaled $285 million.

If the Robert Wood Johnson Foundation were a business, its tax bill each of those years could have been more than $30 million. The foundation actually paid $2.64 million in excise taxes each year, the equivalent of 1 percent of the income.

Last year, the foundation's assets declined to $3.7 billion, said controller G. Russell Henshaw. It awarded $221 million in grants—a record. Nevertheless, that payout amounted to just six cents on every asset dollar.

Shouldn't a foundation pay out more? "You can argue it both ways," Schroeder said. "I'm not convinced as to the answer."

He described it this way: "You have to ask yourself, well when is the next AIDS epidemic coming? Or when is the bottom going to drop out? We'll face that more, if and when our assets decline, than in times of growth. If an exceptional opportunity comes up . . . we'll go past the 5 percent. Five percent is an operational standard."

Although some critics say foundations should distribute their

10 Largest Foundations*

Not adjusted
for inflation.

FOUNDATION	ASSETS	GIVING[†]	GRA AS PE OF AS
		1991	
1 Ford	$ 6,253,006,737	$ 240,875,343	4ς
2 W.K. Kellogg	5,396,889,094	153,942,541	3ς
3 Robert Wood Johnson	4,081,388,000	123,268,000	3ς
4 Lilly Endowment Inc.	3,592,519,250	131,309,773	4ς
5 John D. and Catherine T. MacArthur	3,393,492,922	122,991,197	4ς
6 Pew Charitable Trusts	3,338,048,594	109,264,608	3ς
7 Rockefeller	2,171,548,237	86,906,769	4ς
8 Andrew W. Mellon	1,701,863,355	86,871,015	5ς
9 Robert W. Woodruff	1,495,171,323	33,372,418	2ς
10 Annenberg	1,477,010,631	53,374,300	4ς
Top 10 total	**$32,900,938,143**	**$1,142,175,964**	**3ς**

* Does not include J. Paul Getty Trust, an operating foundation that runs a museum.
[†]Awards made, not all disbursed that year.
SOURCE: Foundation Center and Robert Wood Johnson Foundation

money for the purpose intended and go out of business, the
trustees of the Johnson Foundation, created in 1972, view it as a
permanent entity. Besides making grants, the goal is to pre-
serve the foundation's "corpus," or core assets, so it can survive, even in the face of inflation.

Doing that, Schroeder said, is more difficult than just keep-
ing pace with the overall inflation rate. Inflation in health care,
the foundation's area of interest, has been running about twice
the overall consumer rate. "We can't keep up with health-care
inflation anyhow," he said. If the foundation spent down its
assets, "we'd have less of a chance."

	1990		CHANGE BETWEEN 1990-1991	
ASSETS	GIVING†	GRANTS AS PERCENT OF ASSETS	ASSETS	GRANTS
60,896,289	$ 227,828,194	4%	15%	6%
09,461,224	121,974,324	3%	54%	26%
14,183,000	76,760,000	3%	40%	61%
43,648,222	107,930,515	3%	1%	22%
77,581,000	115,675,981	4%	10%	6%
76,891,792	155,113,636	5%	8%	–30%
71,970,559	84,723,570	4%	10%	3%
17,441,434	74,467,370	5%	5%	17%
95,893,546	26,448,425	3%	50%	26%
96,093,214	59,559,779	5%	23%	–10%
64,060,280	$1,050,481,794	4%	20%	9%

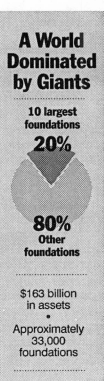

A World Dominated by Giants

10 largest foundations

20%

80%
Other foundations

$163 billion in assets
•
Approximately 33,000 foundations

The Philadelphia Inquirer

Increasing their wealth year after year has had another effect. Foundations have become an industry, requiring layers of well-paid executives, managers, investment advisers, and trustees.

Joanne Sage and Helen Pariza sit face-to-face in a crowded Manhattan office, surrounded by colorful computer screens flashing stock prices and up-to-the-minute financial news. Fifteen telephone lines ring automatically into major brokerage houses, with brokers on the other end waiting to hear "buy" or "sell."

With thirteen other financial professionals, Sage and Pariza are responsible for the care and feeding of more than $6 billion in assets. They nurture a stock portfolio of more than fifty million shares in about one hundred companies. Colleagues have other duties, from analyzing the potential of specific companies to managing billions of dollars in bonds.

These professionals have done a good job: In the last ten years, the assets have more than doubled. They have grown by nearly three times the consumer inflation rate.

This could be a success story for a large mutual fund. Or the tale of some hot Wall Street traders. But it's not. This is the Ford Foundation, the nation's largest grant maker, most often associated with charitable programs aimed at poverty, education, and health around the world.

At the Ford Foundation, everything is big. Its twelve-story glass-and-steel headquarters in New York surrounds a lush, one-third-acre garden under a skylight 160 feet above. The foundation's 607-page 1991 tax filing is five inches thick. While 2½ inches are devoted to grants, two inches detail one year of capital gains and losses in trading securities.

The highest-paid employees at the Ford Foundation in 1991—not including officers and directors—were those responsible for making sure the assets continue to multiply. Richard Hopkins, the highest-paid employee that year, received $414,298 in salary and benefits as director of fixed-income investments; Linda Strumpf received $410,402 as director of equity investments, and Allen Faurot was paid $333,109 as director of special investments.

The Ford Foundation, established by Henry and Edsel Ford in 1936, today is the nation's wealthiest foundation and the grand-daddy of grant makers. In 1991, Ford distributed $241 million—an amount 57 percent larger than second-ranked W.K. Kellogg Foundation. Even though it wrote checks for hundreds of millions of dollars, Ford's grants still amounted to only 4 percent of its assets.

In size of assets, here's how the Top Ten foundations rank as of 1991:

1. *Ford Foundation, $6.3 billion.*
2. *W.K. Kellogg Foundation, $5.4 billion.*
3. *Robert Wood Johnson Foundation, $4.1 billion.*
4. *Lilly Endowment, $3.6 billion.*
5. *John D. and Catherine T. MacArthur Foundation, $3.4 billion.*

6. *Pew Charitable Trusts, $3.3 billion.*
7. *Rockefeller Foundation, $2.2 billion.*
8. *Andrew W. Mellon Foundation, $1.7 billion.*
9. *Robert W. Woodruff Foundation, $1.5 billion.*
10. *Annenberg Foundation, $1.5 billion.*

The ranking is according to the 1993 edition of the *Foundation Directory,* published by the Foundation Center in New York City. Not included is the J. Paul Getty Trust ($4.8 billion), which operates the J. Paul Getty Museum in Los Angeles but distributes few grants.

In the latest fiscal year, 1992, Kellogg and Ford were neck and neck for the distinction of wealthiest foundation. Kellogg's assets, most of it in Kellogg Company stock, reached $6.45 billion. Ford's assets were $6.47 billion.

Their wealth has made foundations such as Ford, Rockefeller, Kellogg, and Robert Wood Johnson among the nation's most economically powerful institutions. How they vote their stock—and where they invest their money—carry great weight on Wall Street and in corporate boardrooms.

Because many foundations were established with large blocks of donated stock, they have had significant influence and control over some of the largest corporations. A 1972 congressional study, the first to try to assess the effect of tax-exempt foundations on the economy, said: "There is reason for concern when such power is held by a relatively small and select group who can perpetuate themselves in office, and who never have to face the scrutiny of a public that is affected daily by their autonomous action."

The Internal Revenue Service has defined a foundation as a "private, nonprofit organization with a narrow base of financial support whose goal is to maintain or assist social, educational, religious, or other activities deemed to serve the public good." That narrow base has narrowed even more.

As their income has grown, the larger foundations have come to rely less on contributions from the public. They have become self-sustaining, no longer needing benefactors. In 1990, the Ford Foundation, for example, received no contributions or gifts, its tax return shows. The foundation earned $55 million in interest on savings and $259 million on dividends. It paid out $237 million that year in charitable grants.

Similarly, the Robert Wood Johnson Foundation received just

$15 in contributions in 1991. It made $267 million in interest, dividends, and capital gains; it handed out $93.5 million in grants.

Only about one-fifth of the revenue of large foundations came from contributions in 1989, whereas smaller ones depended on donations for two-thirds of their revenues.

There is another difference between large and smaller foundations: their generosity. The largest foundations give out the least in proportion to their wealth. In 1989, foundations with $100 million or more in assets paid out exactly 5 percent, according to an Internal Revenue Service study. The smallest foundations, those with less than $100,000 in assets, paid out about 11 percent. The overall average was 7 percent.

The IRS study found that in 1989, large foundations gave away in charity an amount equal to one-half of their investment income. In contrast, smaller foundations gave away twice as much as their investments earned. Smaller ones often act as a conduit, turning contributions they receive into grants.

Congress periodically has become concerned about the financial control over United States businesses exerted by foundations through their stock holdings. Over the years, members of Congress have proposed a number of changes in the law. Many of the proposals were ignored; in some cases, stricter rules that did get adopted later were softened.

Although foundations have accomplished much good, altruism was not always the motivation behind their founding. Many were established as tax shelters—a means of preserving a family's or corporation's wealth by shielding stock from inheritance or income taxes while retaining voting control over those shares.

Even before the income tax was adopted in 1913, official Washington was eyeing the foundations that had been set up by corporate chieftains and worrying whether they would become mere repositories of wealth. A congressional commission in 1912 recommended that foundations be required to distribute all their income every year. They would not have been required to pay out more than 10 percent of their assets.

As Congress was developing income tax law between 1913 and 1917, there was some concern that taxing incomes would cause people to cut their charitable giving. So philanthropic organizations were exempted by Congress and taxpayers were permitted to deduct their gifts to these organizations. Through the deduction, an IRS study says, "the federal government effectively subsidizes charitable activities."

In 1934, tax-exempt foundations were prohibited from lobbying. In 1943, foundations and other tax-exempt groups were ordered to begin filing informational tax returns, even though they were exempt from income taxes. And in 1950, several regulations were imposed on foundations, including ones governing the taxing of business income unrelated to their exempt purpose and public disclosure of their finances.

An issue debated for some time had been whether tax-exempt foundations should be allowed to become self-perpetuating charities or should be required, in effect, to spend themselves out of business. An advisory committee in 1954 said a foundation's life should be kept to ten to twenty-five years. All income would have to be distributed in two to three years. That recommendation never became law.

Fifteen years later, when Congress was considering the Tax Reform Act of 1969, it was proposed that a foundation should have a tax-exempt life of no more than forty years. That didn't make it into law, either.

Congress was sufficiently concerned about the power and influence of foundations in 1969 to attempt to rein them in. That year, lawmakers required foundations each year to give away either their net income or 6 percent of their assets, whichever was greater. The 6 percent floor for distributions was cut to 5 percent in 1976.

The 1969 law also prohibited foundations from owning more than 20 percent of the voting stock in any corporation, except for those that already owned a larger share. Before 1969, there had been no minimum payout requirements, although the IRS could revoke a foundation's tax exemption if the agency believed it wasn't giving away enough. The IRS "rarely applied this penalty due to its severity," an IRS study says.

The lack of monitoring of foundations was called a "major loophole in our system of taxation" by a 1972 study released by the House Banking Committee. The Internal Revenue Service was chastised for its "laxity" in carrying out its responsibility.

The study also found that "many of these private foundations have been used as a vehicle for perpetrating control over a substantial portion of our nation's wealth by a select few, chosen for financial status or prestige rather than democratic means."

To pay for better monitoring by the IRS, Congress imposed a 4 percent excise tax on foundations' investment income in 1969. By 1978, the tax had been cut to 2 percent, and in 1985 foundations were allowed to begin paying only 1 percent if their grants reached the 5 percent threshold. Nevertheless, some foundation executives say they have received too much attention from Congress and the IRS.

"Congress does not like private philanthropic foundations, and, in all likelihood, never will," wrote Terrance Keenan, a longtime official of the Robert Wood Johnson Foundation, in a booklet published in September 1992 examining the prospects for foundations in the 1990s. In a section titled "The Rocky Road of Regulation," Keenan wrote that although Congress is subject to public accountability, it "is very uncomfortable with the foundation as a center of power and wealth which has no such accountability. The congressional hostility toward foundations has been manifest since the passage of federal income tax legislation."

When visitors arrive to meet with executives on the twenty-third floor of the Freedom Forum's headquarters in Arlington, Virginia, it's hard to avoid being distracted. A large, plush anteroom, with sofas, chairs, and a huge wood-burning fireplace, draws you in. A wall of windows offers a panorama of the nation's capital.

To one side is the office of Charles L. Overby, the Freedom Forum's president. To the other side is the office of Allen H. Neuharth, the foundation's chairman. One wall of the reception room is covered with framed photographs of Neuharth, smiling and greeting a variety of world leaders.

In the foundation business, it costs a lot to give away money. And few foundations spend more giving it away than the Freedom Forum and Al Neuharth. So much, in fact, that it is under scrutiny by the New York Attorney General's Office, which is investigating whether its expenditures have been excessive.

The Freedom Forum, formerly called the Gannett Foundation, is a major funder of journalism programs. In fiscal year 1992, it spent $1.71 in administrative costs for every $1 spent in contributions, gifts, or grants, according to its tax filing for that year. That was eight times more than the average for all foundations—twenty cents in administrative costs for every dollar in grants.

The Freedom Forum had $698.5 million in assets in 1992. Administrative expenses totaled $34.4 million; grants and gifts were $20.2 million. Tax records show that in three years, administrative costs grew from thirty-six cents for every grant dollar (1988) to $1.14 (1989) to $1.18 in 1990.

In that period, the foundation moved from Rochester, New York, where it was created in 1935 by newspaper publisher Frank Gannett, to new headquarters it leases on the top three floors and the rooftop of a glass tower across the Potomac from the capital. The foundation also built a high-tech rooftop conference center, featuring a wall of video screens and elaborate production equipment. Often, executives in Arlington meet via video teleconferences with officials of the foundation's study centers in New York and Nashville.

An analysis of the Freedom Forum's tax filings shows that between 1989 and 1992, spending on salaries doubled; spending on pensions and benefits nearly tripled; occupancy expenses nearly quadrupled; and spending on travel and conferences quadrupled. The board of trustees has held meetings in Hawaii and Puerto Vallarta, Mexico, where forum officers met with Mexico's president. In May 1992, Neuharth and other officers and trustees went on a fact-finding mission to Russia to show support for a free press there.

Neuharth, sixty-nine, former chief executive of Gannett Company, which publishes *USA Today* and other newspapers, was paid $131,000 as head of the foundation in 1992. John C. Quinn, sixty-seven, a former Gannett Company executive, was paid $110,708 as part-time vice-chairman. Neuharth and Quinn live on the same street in Cocoa Beach, Florida. Overby, forty-six, the foundation's president, who is also a former Gannett executive, received $278,040.

Executives of the foundation have said that its mission has changed substantially over the years. Instead of awarding grants in cities where the Gannett Company has newspapers, as it once did, the foundation now spends most of its money funding media-study centers at Columbia and Vanderbilt universities and sponsoring conferences. Neither Freedom Forum officials nor the New York Attorney General's Office would discuss the investigation.

At the rapidly growing John S. and James L. Knight Foundation, president Creed C. Black, sixty-seven, is a former publisher of the Lexington (Kentucky) *Herald-Leader,* owned by Knight-Ridder Newspapers. Black was paid $247,584 in 1991. (The newspaper group includes *The Philadelphia Inquirer.*)

The foundation, established in 1950 by the Knight brothers, has assets of more than $700 million. In 1991 it made grants totaling $25 million to schools, museums, and social welfare groups, many in communities where Knight-Ridder has newspapers. The Knight Foundation's administrative expenses that year, $5 million, were the equivalent of twenty cents for each dollar paid out in grants.

Large foundations typically spend between fifteen and forty cents in administrative expenses for every dollar in grants, IRS filings show. The average spent in 1990 was about twenty cents for every grant dollar, according to data provided by the Foundation Center.

Salaries and benefits traditionally have been an area "where the potential for abuse is great," the pioneering 1972 congressional study on foundations said. That study found that foundations on average were spending fifty cents on administration for every $1 in grants. "The cost of producing and distributing charitable benefits by private foundations is staggering by any standard," the study said. "When funds that are intended for charity are selfishly and wastefully diverted to the administration and management of these foundations, it is charity that is being cheated," it said.

Today, a large share of administrative costs goes to investment advisers and consultants. At the Ford Foundation, in addition to the highly paid in-house money managers, outside investment firms also collected large amounts. The five highest-paid consultants ranged from Templeton Investment Council of Atlanta, which was paid $476,823, to Baring International Investment of London, which received $889,458. In all, Ford Foundation's annual report says "expenses incurred in the production of income" in 1990 totaled $14.7 million.

n 1991, foundations paid out $9.2 billion in grants. What did they get for their money?

At the Ford Foundation, projects ranged from a $46,300 grant for a program to help low-income Camden, N.J., residents commute to work to a $5.1 million academic grant to the National Academy of Science for doctoral minority fellowship programs.

"There are a lot of good projects out there and we can't fund all of them," said Barry Gaberman, deputy vice-president of the Ford Foundation's program division, which is in charge of spending the foundation's money. In 1992, the Ford Foundation received thirty-three thousand grant requests and made seventeen hundred grants, for a total of $276.5 million.

When foundations are formed, their benefactors don't always stipulate how the money is to be spent. In some cases, grants are focused on specific problem areas. Robert Wood Johnson aims at health-care problems.

In 1991, the Robert Wood Johnson Foundation made a $1.3 million, three-year grant to the state of Indiana to develop affordable long-term health insurance for the elderly. A three-year grant of $1.5 million went to Children's Hospital of Philadelphia for a West Philadelphia collaborative program for child health care. And a three-year grant of $139,799 went to the Aroostook Micmac Council in Presque Isle, Maine, to support a health-care program for Native Americans.

The largest single grants from foundations in recent years have included $75 million from the W.M. Keck Foundation to California Institute of Technology for a ten-meter telescope in Hawaii, $9 million from the William Penn Foundation to support the Philadelphia Ranger Corps' work in the city's parks, and $7.5 million from the Andrew W. Mellon Foundation to endow three professionals at the National Gallery of Art in Washington.

And then there are the truly unusual foundations. Like the one named for Harriet DeTrampe of Haverford, Pennsylvania, who died at age 101. In her will, she made provisions for the Countess deTrampe Home for Unwanted Dogs in Green Lane, Pa. Today the foundation has $2.3 million in assets and maintains a home for about twenty-five dogs whose elderly owners either had died or had gone to a nursing home.

Some foundations promote religious views or work to influence public opinion. Arthur S. DeMoss was a Christian evangelist who founded National Liberty Life Insurance Company, a

Valley Forge mail-order insurance firm, which he sold in 1979. That also was the year DeMoss, who was fifty-three, died on his tennis court at his Bryn Mawr, Pennsylvania, mansion.

DeMoss had set up a foundation in St. Davids, Pennsylvania, to "promulgate the Christian gospel throughout the world by any and all proper means." In 1992, the tax-exempt foundation funded a controversial television ad campaign promoting adoption for expectant mothers who didn't want to keep their babies. The ads, "Life: What a Beautiful Choice," aired on national television and were widely viewed as being anti-abortion. The advertising campaign was a major endeavor for DeMoss, which had assets of more than $400 million in 1991.

Control of the foundation remains with seven family members. They are led by Arthur's widow, Nancy S. DeMoss, who was paid $136,825 in 1991 to serve as chairwoman and chief executive officer.

In the case of the Annenberg Foundation, the primary mission is to fund communications schools at the University of Pennsylvania and the University of Southern California. Many schools receive large donations from benefactors, with the understanding that they will be used for specific programs. But the Annenberg Foundation has a role in actually operating the communications schools at the private universities.

"The universities and the foundation jointly operate schools for the purpose of providing instruction in communication in radio, television, and in other media," the foundation's 1991 tax filing says. Although the Annenberg School's dean, Kathleen Jamieson, reports to Penn's administration, she is listed on the Annenberg Foundation's tax filing as its highest-paid employee— with compensation of $214,723.

Four other professors from Penn and USC are listed as receiving pay packages of more than $100,000. Half the members of the Annenberg School's board of trustees come from the foundation; the others are from Penn.

The foundation, based in St. Davids, is run by Walter H. Annenberg, former ambassador to Great Britain and former owner of *The Inquirer.* In 1992, its assets were $1.4 billion, making it the tenth largest grant-making foundation.

As president of the foundation, Annenberg was paid $150,000 in 1991, according to the tax filing. His office in St. Davids also received $350,000 from the foundation for professional services, which included investment accounting and administration. In addition to the communications schools, the foundation gave to other causes.

In 1991, the foundation contributed $5.9 million to operate Penn's Annenberg School and $4.4 million to USC. It is a "unique funding mechanism," John W. Gould, acting executive vice-president at Penn, said of the school's relationship to the foundation. Someday, he said, Penn officials hope the school will be endowed.

O ne reason for creating a foundation with a bequest is to do good. Another is to reduce a tax bill. Yet another, said Schroeder of the Robert Wood Johnson Foundation, is to build a "monument." This monument isn't carved from stone. It's built with dollars.

It is this monument factor that worries Schroeder when he hears talk about stiffer tax rates on foundations or proposals to limit the life of foundations to only ten or twenty years. "I could have a ball spending the next ten years wiping out this $3.4 billion. Don't get me wrong. I think it would be an incredible thing to do," he said. But rules limiting foundations could put a damper on philanthropy, Schroeder said.

"To the extent that donors give partly to have a monument to themselves or their family, and you create disincentives to do that, then you turn down the spigot, or turn off the spigot, on the bequesting of philanthropic wealth," he said.

But to some, a generous yet short-lived foundation isn't such a bad idea. In fact, those were the orders in the will of multimillionaire Lucille P. Markey, who died in 1982.

Markey's family fortune came from the Calumet Baking Powder Company and, later, Calumet Farm—a leading breeder of thoroughbred horses. Markey and her husband had many Kentucky Derby winners and invested in oil and gas, which turned into millions.

Before Markey died in Miami she wrote her will and was precise in her wishes for what today is the Lucille P. Markey Charitable Trust. This trust, which started out with $250 million, should last no longer than fifteen years after her death, she stipulated.

Markey was a private woman and wanted to make sure how

her money was spent, said Nancy W. Weber, the foundation's director of program administration. "She wanted people she knew to manage the trust," and named them in her will, Weber said.

The philanthropist wanted the money to go for basic medical research. She knew that some long-lasting foundations had been formed to find a cure for a disease, and after a cure was discovered, the foundation had to find something else to do with the money. "She did not want her money to outlive the purpose," Weber said.

As of 1992, the Markey Trust had $169 million left. New grants totaling $56.5 million were authorized. The relatively low-budget trust, which operates with ten employees in a former Miami law office (the trust bought the law firm's used furniture when the firm moved out), will be out of business in 1997.

Too modest an end for a generous benefactor? Not at all, Weber said. "She did not want this big organization or buildings named after her."

CHAPTER 9

Finding out on your own

The growth of America's public charities and nonprofit organizations has given rise to a culture of secrecy that rivals that of the most private companies. Ask a large charity or nonprofit to see a copy of its tax return and you may be told the following:

- Write us a letter stating why you want to see it.
- How about if we send you a copy of our annual report instead?
- We don't have to show it to you.
- You can see it, but you can't write about it without our permission.

"It is my understanding that you will not use the name of our organization without obtaining prior approval from the executive director," Darcy E. Wertz of the nonprofit organization U.S. English advised a *Philadelphia Inquirer* reporter who had asked for the group's IRS filing.

The tax-exempt purpose of U.S. English? It advocates English as the nation's official language. Wertz is the group's human resources manager.

Whatever they tell you, stand your ground: Any citizen has a right to know what's in the tax filing of a nonprofit organization.

Federal law requires nonprofit groups to show to anyone who asks for it their original application for tax-exempt status, as

well as the last three years of their informational tax return
known as a Form 990. These documents must be kept on file at
the organization's offices for public inspection. Individuals also
may request copies of 990s by writing to the IRS. (Addresses
for IRS regional offices are listed later in this chapter.)

As part of these filings, charities must list the salaries and
benefits of the five highest paid officers and directors earning
more than $30,000 a year. Another part of the form calls for the
five highest paid employees. Yet another asks for the five high
est paid consultants.

These disclosure requirements are supposed to serve as a
check in the government's otherwise meager oversight of non
profit groups. "There will always be more organizations than
the IRS and state attorneys general can keep tabs on," said
Marcus S. Owens, director of the IRS's Exempt Organizations
Technical Division. "By making the 990s available, it was hoped
that the spotlight of publicity would serve as a kind of a check."

It doesn't always work that way. Many tax-exempt groups
resist when it comes to revealing details about their finances
especially executive salaries and perks. They've discovered a
multitude of tactics to divert, or even subvert, the curiosity and
interest of citizens. These tactics include leaving crucial infor
mation blank on the IRS forms; refusing to provide returns to
people who ask for them; and shifting management functions to
private, profit-making firms to avoid disclosure.

For example, under state law, Independence Blue Cross of
Pennsylvania is considered a nonprofit organization and pays
no income tax, sales tax, or insurance premium tax. Yet officials
refuse to provide any information about the compensation paid
to their top executives.

"These returns contain highly confidential and competitively
sensitive business information, the disclosure of which could
impact negatively on the business initiatives of Independence
Blue Cross," general counsel Patricia R. Hatler wrote in re
sponse to a 1989 request for information.

Court records show that former Blue Cross president David
S. Markson was paid $495,000 in salary and bonuses in 1987
Other Blue Cross and Blue Shield executives nationwide receive
salaries ranging from $300,000 to more than $750,000, state
insurance records show.

Another tax-exempt group that declines to disclose salary

information for key officers is the Allegheny General Hospital
group, which controls Medical College Hospitals in Philadelphia. In 1988, the Pittsburgh organization set up a separate
corporation, Centennial Health Services, to pay executives and
handle other management functions. Although incorporated as
a nonprofit organization, Centennial pays federal and state taxes.
As a result, Centennial does not have to make its tax return
public, an attorney said. A hospital spokesman said the information is considered "privileged."

The situation is similar at Quakertown Community Hospital in
Bucks County, outside Philadelphia. The small, nonprofit hospital is managed by American Health Resources Systems, a profit-
making firm that employs seven top executives of the hospital.

What if a citizen of Quakertown wanted to check those salaries? "We are a private institution. We consider payroll private," Michael Hammond, Quakertown's administrator in 1992,
said. He has since left the company.

Some large nonprofits file returns with the IRS and state
regulators but omit information on officers' and directors' salaries. For example, Hadassah, a tax-exempt Jewish women's
service group based in New York City, wrote on its 1990 IRS
return that salary information "is confidential and will be sup-
plied [only] upon request." The United States Golf Association
in Far Hills, New Jersey, took a similar approach.

Planned Parenthood Federation of America noted that five
employees were paid between $121,192 and $200,000 each. It
left out their names on its IRS return. The Museum of Modern
Art in Manhattan lumped together the salaries of its highest
paid officers and employees but failed to disclose individual
salaries in a return filed with the IRS. A return on file at the
museum contained salary data. Ducks Unlimited, a conserva-
tion group, listed benefits but not salaries, in a 990 return filed
in New Jersey.

Owens said the IRS position was that the information on
salaries and loans made to executives by nonprofits must be
disclosed in the forms. "It has to be public," he said. Then how
do incomplete filings slip by? The federal agency has fewer than
five hundred employees to monitor the half-million Form 990s
filed annually by charities and other nonprofits. Most returns
are never examined. Organizations can skirt disclosure rules
with virtual immunity.

IRS officials acknowledged as much during a 1991 congressional hearing. "I can tell you that we routinely attend health law seminars throughout this country. We have on many occasions listened to presentations from tax practitioners advising those who attend the seminar how best to avoid the requirements," said James J. McGovern, IRS associate chief counsel.

Some executives at large nonprofit groups apparently are not familiar with federal disclosure requirements. When a reporter told Frankford Hospital president John B. Neff that the hospital's Form 990 excluded his salary, Neff said, "I don't know these forms. I never see them. I'm going to play dumb and say I've never paid attention to it. I don't have a clue."

Officials at Franklin Square Hospital in Philadelphia couldn't find their own tax return. "At present, I haven't located it," Charles Carlson, the hospital's chief financial officer, said.

Thomas A. Sullivan, treasurer of the National Football League, initially told a reporter the nonprofit didn't have to make its IRS returns public. After reviewing the law, Sullivan reversed himself. "Thank you for making us aware of the law," he said. "No one ever asked us before. We really didn't know what we were required to do. Now we know."

Where to write for a copy of a nonprofit's 990 tax form

The nonprofit organization's tax filing, called a Form 990, is a public document. The organization is required to allow members of the public to review its 990 filings for the three most recent years, although the organization does not have to make a photocopy for you.

However, you can order copies from the Internal Revenue Service. Usually there is no charge. Be advised that it can take several months to get the information. And there may be a lag of several months before a tax filing is available if the organization has asked for and received deadline extensions from the IRS.

For photocopies of 990s write to the IRS regional center that covers the state in which the nonprofit organization is headquartered. Provide the name and city of the organization; if at all possible, also try to provide the street address and employer identification number. However, if that isn't possible, the name and city will do.

New England/Mid-Atlantic States

For Maine, New Hampshire, Vermont, Massachusetts, Rhode Island, Connecticut, New York, and New Jersey:

Internal Revenue Service
Brookhaven Service Center
Stop No. 532
P.O. Box 400
Holtsville, NY 11742

Mid-Atlantic, Puerto Rico, International

For Pennsylvania, Delaware, Maryland, District of Columbia, Puerto Rico, and international:

Internal Revenue Service
Philadelphia Service Center
Attn. Photocopy Unit
DP 536
11511 Roosevelt Blvd.
Philadelphia, PA 19154

South

For Alabama, Arkansas, Florida, Georgia, Mississippi, North Carolina, South Carolina, Tennessee, and Louisiana:

Internal Revenue Service
Atlanta Service Center
Stop 350
P.O. Box 47421
Atlanta, GA 30362

Midwest

For Ohio, West Virginia, Michigan, Indiana, and Kentucky:

Internal Revenue Service
Cincinnati Service Center
Stop 524
P.O. Box 145500
Cincinnati, OH 45214

Midwest/Plains

For Missouri, Illinois, Iowa, Wisconsin, Minnesota, Montana, Nebraska, North Dakota, and South Dakota:

Internal Revenue Service
Kansas City Service Center
P.O. Box 24551
Kansas City, MO 64131

Southwest, West

For Texas, Kansas, Oklahoma, Arizona, New Mexico, Utah, Colorado, and Wyoming:

Internal Revenue Service
Austin Service Center
Stop 7000
P.O. Box 934
Austin, TX 78767

Far West, Alaska, Hawaii

For California, Hawaii, Alaska, Oregon, Washington, Idaho, and Nevada:

Internal Revenue Service
Fresno Service Center
Attn. Disclosure Officer
P.O. Box 12866
Fresno, CA 93779

EPILOGUE

The line began to form early outside the small hearing room in the basement of the Rayburn House Office Building in Washington, D.C. It quickly snaked down the long, narrow hallway and then around a corner and down another hall.

By 1 P.M., the time the hearing was scheduled to start, guards were warning many of the well-dressed lawyers, accountants, lobbyists, and executives that there might not be room for them inside.

Behind Room B-318's closed doors, staff of the House Ways and Means Subcommittee on Oversight shuffled stacks of documents, newspaper clippings, and press handouts. A technician checked a recording device. A small cadre of IRS officials, including newly appointed commissioner Margaret Milner Richardson, exchanged small talk and nervous laughter. Richardson and her colleagues had been allowed in early to avoid the crush. It was a small show of courtesy by the subcommittee, which would spend the next two hours relentlessly grilling the government officials.

It was June 15, 1993, nearly two months after the newspaper series *Warehouses of Wealth: The Tax-Free Economy* had been published in *The Philadelphia Inquirer*. About to begin was the first of a series of hearings on abuses within the nonprofit economy. The hearing had been called by the subcommittee's chairman, J.J. Pickle, a populist Texas Democrat with a knack for cutting through the verbal gymnastics of witnesses with plain-speaking humor.

After years of tinkering with the tax code while financial abuses grew, Congress finally appeared ready to take on the nonprofits. The tax-exempt economy had grown so large that it threatened "to get bigger than the government," Pickle said in his opening.

Drawing on data reported in the *Inquirer,* Pickle noted that there were now more than 1.2 million tax-exempt organizations, not including an estimated 340,000 churches, with revenue of $500 billion a year and assets of approximately $1 trillion.

"Once a tax-exempt organization gets on the books, it normally stays there forever," Pickle said. "They last longer than the stars."

That growth had spawned many problems for regulators, he said, which was why the subcommittee had called in the IRS to testify.

"Due to the growth in the number, size, and complex operations of public charities, serious questions exist about whether the Internal Revenue Service has been able to keep pace," he said. Pickle pointed out that the IRS's Exempt Organizations Division "has fewer employees today monitoring nonprofits than in 1980; funding continues to decline, and the number of tax-exempt audits performed by IRS has dropped sharply."

Hamstrung by its inability to levy penalties short of revoking a nonprofit's tax exemption, the vaunted tax agency had become a paper tiger, subcommittee members observed. And the lack of any meaningful oversight, in turn, had opened the door to increasing abuses.

Pickle ticked off a few—without naming any names—that had been compiled by the staff:

- A no-interest, fifty-year loan of $1 million by a university to its president to buy and renovate a house. The president also received $365,000 a year in compensation. "The Lord's taking care of him," Pickle said.
- A nonprofit hospital that made $1.5 million in loans to officers and directors, including an $845,000 loan to its director of surgery.
- A university that hired a Washington lobbyist for $600,000,

and two other tax-exempt universities that paid a total of $650,000 to the same lobbyist.

■ A university that earned $196 million in profits yet collected $127 million in tuition the same year. Students ought to be allowed to attend the school for free for a year and a half, Pickle said.

IRS officials acknowledged that the number of abuses had grown, although they quickly added that most nonprofits operate in an appropriate way. Most of the abuses uncovered by revenue agents during audits involved cases of executives taking advantage of their positions to enrich themselves through big salaries, no-interest loans, luxury cars, and other perks, IRS officials testified.

In one instance, Richardson said, the agency had revoked the tax exemption of an organization—retroactively—after it purchased a forty-two-foot boat for the personal use of an executive.

But revocations are the exception, not the rule, the testimony indicated. In the 1980s, the IRS pulled the exemptions of an average of about thirty public charities a year. Yet it approved approximately thirty thousand new nonprofits a year during that time. The threat of revocation was just that—a threat, said Pickle.

"I think the only way you are going to straighten out this huge advance of tax-exempt organizations" is by penalizing abuses, Pickle told IRS officials. "This business of examining it and massaging it and reordering the foo-foo of it, is not going to do it. We've got to do something about it, rather than just say it."

"And I don't disagree with any of those things," responded Richardson. "That's why we're stepping up our enforcement actions. We're very concerned . . ."

"We want to see these abuses minimized and cut down. We have to take action," Pickle said. "Now, I want to know what are the abuses? I want to help you. How can we help you?"

One thing Congress could do, Richardson said, was to give the agency power to impose sanctions less drastic than revoking a nonprofit's tax-exempt status. "Revocation of an exemption is a severe sanction that may be greatly disproportional to the violation in issue," Richardson said.

Pickle responded that the subcommittee would examine drafting legislation giving the IRS such sanctions. He also suggested

:he agency could use more staff. But IRS officials downplayed
:he need for more investigators; that could cause "growing
pains," Assistant IRS Commissioner John E. Burke said.

Growing pains shouldn't be a concern, Pickle replied heat-
edly. "I find that unacceptable. I would think that common
sense would tell you that you've got to have more people and
you've got to attack the problem with vigor."

During that first hearing, subcommittee members identified
several other steps they would explore to increase oversight of
nonprofit organizations. They include:

- Publicizing penalties and other regulatory actions taken
  against nonprofits. Now these actions are kept secret, unless the nonprofit consents to their release. "We think that
  type of disclosure would be helpful," Richardson said.
- Making tax forms of nonprofit organizations more readily
  available to the public. At present, interested consumers
  must write to the IRS or visit a nonprofit's office to see its
  tax returns. The subcommittee might require tax-exempt
  organizations to mail copies of their returns to people who
  request them, for a small fee.
- Expanding the information currently in nonprofit tax returns to include more details about executive compensation, about business dealings between nonprofits and their
  board members, and about for-profit subsidiaries and spinoff companies created by nonprofits.
- Establishing limits on salaries and pay packages of executives of public charities. Charities would either have to get
  IRS approval to pay more or possibly pay a tax for exceeding the approved amount.
- Requiring nonprofit groups to reapply for their tax exemption every five or ten years. Now, once an exemption is
  granted, it lasts indefinitely.
- And, if necessary, placing a freeze on new applications in
  order to slow the growth of tax-exempt groups.

Which, if any, of these proposed changes will be adopted
remains in question. Subcommittee staff members acknowledge
the power and persuasiveness of the nonprofits lobby.

"We know we are up against it," one staffer said. "Most of
these groups have access to Congress . . . and your typical
congressman doesn't want to take on nonprofits. You don't win
anything doing that."

Nevertheless, this time there's one important difference, the staffers say. "There's a wide perception even among the non profits that something has to be done. They don't want the entire nonprofit sector being punished for a few bad apples."

Some form of legislation will almost certainly be introduced "We just must do a better job," Pickle said.

IRS officials said they agreed. "The fact is we do need to sit down with your staff and Treasury so that there is much more sunshine, and the public is aware of what's going on," said Burke.

Beyond Capitol Hill, there is also growing interest in the operations of public charities and tax-exempt groups.

In Omaha, Boston, Philadelphia, and Trenton, city officials are considering whether to tax nonprofits. In Boston, a study of that city's prestigious teaching hospitals, commissioned by the local health department, found that the dozen largest teaching hospitals had accumulated more than $1 billion in surplus funds— while health needs were going unmet. The study, released in May 1993, received widespread attention and prompted calls for action by consumer groups and politicians.

In Texas, the legislature passed a law requiring nonprofit hospitals, by 1996, to provide charity care, education, or research equal to at least 4 percent of net patient revenue in return for their exemptions from property, sales, and franchise taxes. The law, signed by Governor Ann Richards in June 1993, followed revelations that some large Texas nonprofit hospitals provided little or no charity care.

All this attention has prompted unprecedented soul-searching within the nonprofit world. *The Chronicle of Philanthropy,* a major publication for charities, on June 15, 1993, published a cover story titled "A Crisis of Credibility for America's Non-Profits." One foundation executive quoted in the six-page article, Rebecca Rimel, executive director of the Pew Charitable Trusts, referred to recent press coverage as "a wake-up call" for non profits. Other executives worried about the loss of public trust and whether donations would dry up.

Some executives have been critical of the press for reporting their pay packages and other business details. Others have called for a new sense of responsibility and openness. "We must recommit ourselves, as a sector, to self-criticism and self-correction," one official wrote. "The question is whether the sector, having systematically discouraged critical and independent scholarship for so long, has this capacity," another official responded.

Indeed, nothing short of the credibility of nonprofits is at stake in the public examination of their privileges and practices. Some tax-exempt groups believe they are under attack and are digging in their heels. Others say the media and congressional scrutiny is long overdue. In the aftermath of the *Inquirer*'s series, a surprising number of nonprofit executives and employees wrote to congratulate the newspaper.

"Although I have spent my entire working life teaching in universities and in successive employment by two 'non-profits,' I share many of the concerns that you have ably described in your articles. I hope that they will be the stimulus for badly needed reforms," one official wrote.

"The series was particularly gratifying to me because I have been for some years in the upper echelons of one of the nonprofit health-care institutions you covered in detail," wrote another official. "And not only can I attest to the accuracy of the thrust of your report, and some of the numbers (although some of your revelations in terms of specific compensations, etc., were news even to me), but I have frequently been morally concerned, and on occasion shocked, at what has been happening. I have on occasion protested some of the directions being taken, but these protests were generally interpreted as either radical ravings or something approaching treason."

"I live in the world you . . . did such a superb job examining," wrote another. "I recognized lots of familiar sights and places—the lavish Ford Foundation headquarters, the highly paid salaries of university surgeons, the rising university tuitions, the grudging provision of free care by hugely profitable conglomerates, and the cushy trips to posh resorts by all manner of charitable organizations. I could only grit my teeth . . ."